FORTRESS • 100

THE FÜHRER'S HEADQUARTERS

Hitler's command bunkers 1939–45

NEIL SHORT

ILLUSTRATED BY ADAM HOOK

Series editor Marcus Cowper

First published in 2010 by Osprey Publishing
Midland House, West Way, Botley, Oxford OX2 0PH, UK
44-02 23rd St, Suite 219, Long Island City, NY 11101, USA

E-mail: info@ospreypublishing.com

A CIP catalogue record for this book is available from the British Library.

ISBN: 978 1 84603 582 1

E-book ISBN: 9 7818 4908 302 7

Editorial by Ilios Publishing Ltd, Oxford, UK (www.iliospublishing.com)
Cartography: Map Studio, Romsey, UK
Page layout by Ken Vail Graphic Design, Cambridge, UK (kvgd.com)
Typeset in Myriad and Sabon
Index by David Worthington
Originated by PDQ Digital Media Solutions Ltd, Suffolk, UK
Printed in China through Bookbuilders

10 11 12 13 14   10 9 8 7 6 5 4 3 2 1

Osprey Publishing are supporting the Woodland Trust, the UK's leading woodland conservation charity, by funding the dedication of trees.

www.ospreypublishing.com

DEDICATION

This book is dedicated to my long-suffering wife, Nikki – a special book for a special person!

ARTIST'S NOTE

Readers may care to note that the original paintings from which the colour plates in this book were prepared are available for private sale. All reproduction copyright whatsoever is retained by the Publishers. All enquiries should be addressed to:

Scorpio Gallery, PO Box 475, Hailsham, East Sussex, BN27 2SL, UK

The Publishers regret that they can enter into no correspondence upon this matter.

THE FORTRESS STUDY GROUP (FSG)

The object of the FSG is to advance the education of the public in the study of all aspects of fortifications and their armaments, especially works constructed to mount or resist artillery. The FSG holds an annual conference in September over a long weekend with visits and evening lectures, an annual tour abroad lasting about eight days, and an annual Members' Day.

The FSG journal *FORT* is published annually, and its newsletter *Casemate* is published three times a year. Membership is international. For further details, please contact:

secretary@fsgfort.com

Website: www.fsgfort.com

THE HISTORY OF FORTIFICATION STUDY CENTRE (HFSC)

The History of Fortification Study Centre (HFSC) is an international scientific research organization that aims to unite specialists in the history of military architecture from antiquity to the 20th century (including historians, art historians, archaeologists, architects and those with a military background). The centre has its own scientific council, which is made up of authoritative experts who have made an important contribution to the study of fortification.

The HFSC's activities involve organizing conferences, launching research expeditions to study monuments of defensive architecture, contributing to the preservation of such monuments, arranging lectures and special courses in the history of fortification and producing published works such as the refereed academic journal *Questions of the History of Fortification*, monographs and books on the history of fortification. It also holds a competition for the best publication of the year devoted to the history of fortification.

The headquarters of the HFSC is in Moscow, Russia, but the centre is active in the international arena and both scholars and amateurs from all countries are welcome to join. More detailed information about the HFSC and its activities can be found on the website: www.hfsc.3dn.ru

E-mail: ciif-info@yandex.ru

ACKNOWLEDGEMENTS

The author would like to thank the many people who helped in the production of this book. In particular Evgeny Hitriak and Ivan Volkov for the information and photographs of *Führerhauptquartiere* in the former Soviet Union, Tom Idzikowski who took me round Anlage Süd in Poland and answered many supplementary questions and Wolfgang Fleischer, who provided photographs of the Führerbunker in Berlin before it was buried for ever.

I would also like to pay especial thanks to my wife and two children, Amy and Lewis, who have proved great travelling partners and have provided much-needed distractions!

AUTHOR'S NOTE

As is so often the case with works on World War II, especially those dealing with the Eastern Front, place names were often changed. For example Rastenburg, formerly in East Prussia, is today found in Poland and known as Ketrzyn. As a general rule place names have been quoted in the German from the period with the contemporary name quoted in brackets.

CONTENTS

THE FÜHRER'S HEADQUARTERS

INTRODUCTION

While researching the history of the Stalin and Molotov Lines for Osprey I was lucky enough to visit a number of the fortified regions of modern-day Poland. While I was there my guide and good friend Tom Idzikowski took me to Stepina and Strzyzów, which are home to two railway tunnels that were used to shelter Hitler's train when he met with Mussolini in August 1941. Little did I know that this entertaining diversion would form a small but important part of my next book.

Anlage Süd, as it was known, was one of more than a dozen *Führerhauptquartiere* (Führer headquarters) built or adapted by the Organisation Todt (OT) for Hitler's personal use between 1939 and the end of the war in 1945. In that time the scale and complexity of Hitler's headquarters grew from a simple air-raid shelter and wooden accommodation blocks to massive concrete bunkers proof against any enemy bomb or shell.

Hitler's obsession with concrete bunkers can be traced back to his time in the trenches during World War I where he served as a *Gefreiter* (corporal) on the Western Front. Here, the only refuges from the constant artillery fire were the deep dugouts, often reinforced with concrete, that were constructed along

Entrance to the concrete rail tunnel at Stepina where Hitler met Mussolini in August 1941. Today the tunnel is used as a museum to house military memorabilia and is open to the public. (Author)

Führerhauptquartiere locations

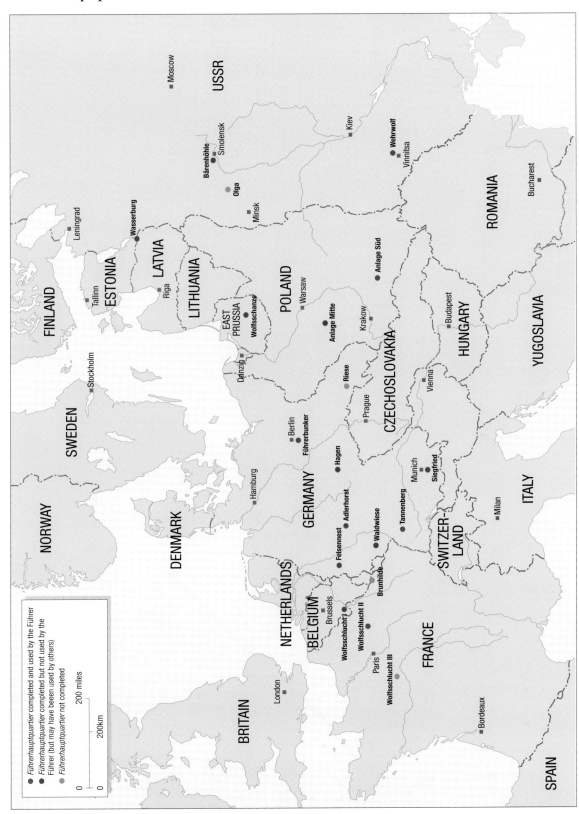

USSR

Moscow

Kiev

Smolensk

Bärenhöhle

Wehrwolf

Vinnitsa

Olga

Minsk

Leningrad

Wasserburg

LATVIA

ESTONIA

FINLAND

Tallinn

Riga

LITHUANIA

EAST PRUSSIA

Wolfsschanze

POLAND

Warsaw

Anlage Süd

Danzig

Krakow

Anlage Mitte

CZECHOSLOVAKIA

Riese

Budapest

HUNGARY

ROMANIA

Bucharest

YUGOSLAVIA

Stockholm

SWEDEN

Prague

Vienna

NORWAY

DENMARK

Hamburg

Berlin

Führerbunker

GERMANY

Hagen

Munich

Siegfried

Felsennest

Adlerhorst

Waldwiese

Tannenberg

SWITZER-LAND

Milan

ITALY

Brunhilde

NETHERLANDS

BELGIUM

Brussels

Wolfsschlucht I

Wolfsschlucht II

FRANCE

Paris

Wolfsschlucht III

London

BRITAIN

Bordeaux

SPAIN

Legend:

● *Führerhauptquartier* completed and used by the Führer

● *Führerhauptquartier* completed but not used by the Führer (but may have beeen used by others)

● *Führerhauptquartier* not completed

0   200 miles

0   200km

the length of the front. Later, as Germany's leader, his preoccupation with concrete fortifications found expression in the decision to construct the Westwall along the border with France and a similar line of defences in the east. Indeed, such was his interest in the subject that he was intimately involved in the design of a number of the bunkers. With no time to build a bespoke headquarters for the invasion of France and the Low Countries, a number of Westwall bunkers were adapted to accommodate Hitler and his staff. However, such was the speed of the German advance that further sites were identified in Belgium and later France so that Hitler was better able to direct operations. With France defeated and Britain isolated Hitler turned his attention east and three more headquarters were built in East Prussia and Poland from where Hitler could oversee the launch of Operation *Barbarossa* – the invasion of the Soviet Union. Once again the German forces enjoyed early success with their blitzkrieg technique and soon further headquarters were planned and built in the Soviet Union.

As the tide of the war turned, however, Hitler was forced to abandon the most distant of these sites, but the turn of events did not slow the pace of construction. Führerhauptquartier Wolfsschanze ('Wolf's Lair') in East Prussia, perhaps the best known of Hitler's headquarters, was extended and the buildings strengthened. More staggeringly, even in these dark days, there were plans to build an even bigger headquarters codenamed FHQ Riese ('Giant') in Silesia, but although work started on this massive project it was never completed. Paradoxically, Hitler ended his days in the Führerbunker – a small, cramped shelter under the Reich Chancellery in Berlin, which was designed not as a headquarters but as a simple air-raid shelter.

This last point raises an interesting question in respect of Hitler's headquarters, specifically: what characterizes a *Führerhauptquartier*? In its narrowest sense it meant that it was used by Hitler, his closest advisers and the Wehrmachtführungsstab (WFSt). However, the definition has been broadened to encompass the headquarters that were built or adapted for Hitler during the war. Technically then, the Berlin bunker was not a *Führerhauptquartier*, but is included in this book because of the pivotal role it played in the final days of the war. The same latitude has not been afforded the likes of the Berghof, which along with Schloß Klessheim, the Königliches Residenzschloß (Royal Palace) at Posen and his accommodation in Munich, was more accurately described as a '*Führerresidenz*'. Furthermore, although 18 *Führerhauptquartiere* were built or planned, Hitler used only nine, and these are the sites that are focused on in this book. The principal exception to this rule is FHQ Riese, which is included because of the sheer scale of the undertaking.

The *Führerhauptquartiere* building programme absorbed enormous amounts of materials and manpower. Most were constructed by the OT, the body responsible for all major infrastructure projects in the Third Reich, but the scale of building was so great that forced labour had to be used more and more frequently, even if it compromised security. Once completed, the headquarters became home to Hitler's entourage of aids, military advisers, cooks, doctors and secretaries. Their life was not glamorous, being confined in poorly ventilated and lit concrete bunkers and where life rotated around Hitler's unusual daily schedule.

As the tide of the war turned, Hitler became increasingly demented and ordered that those *Führerhauptquartiere* in danger of falling into enemy hands should be destroyed. Later, others were demolished by the Allies as part of the denazification programme, or were closed to the public. Still others were lost

After the war Hitler's bunker in Berlin was partially demolished, but in 1988 a decision was taken to remove the last vestiges. The concrete structure was reduced to a tangle of reinforcing rods and lumps of concrete. The I-beams that supported the roof are clearly visible. (W. Fleischer)

behind the Iron Curtain. Now, however, since the thawing of relations between east and west it is possible to visit the various sites, as is true of those in the west, which were previously off limits. The most significant though – the Führerbunker in Berlin – has been lost for ever. A disappointment to students of fortifications, but understandable in a country trying to build a brighter future and consign a difficult chapter in its history to the past.

DESIGN AND DEVELOPMENT

As early as 1924 Hitler laid down his ambitions for territorial gains in his book *Mein Kampf*. At this time though these were little more than pipe dreams, since he was languishing in Landsberg Prison. In the next decade, however, his fortunes improved. In 1933 he was made Chancellor of Germany and following the death of President Hindenburg he became supreme leader, or Führer. Being all-powerful, his ambitions could now begin to be realized. At first his aims were relatively modest: the remilitarization of the Rhineland, *Anschluss* ('union') with Austria and the absorption into the Reich of the Sudeten Germans. Unchecked, he grew in confidence and now annexed the rump of Czechoslovakia, and on 1 September 1939 he took an even greater gamble by invading Poland.

Up until this point the German Army had been greeted as liberators, or at least had not met any resistance. Poland was different. A sovereign state, Poland had always been fearful of her powerful neighbours and had taken steps to defend herself. This, understandably, made Hitler nervous, and, although not at this point in time intimately involved in the planning and direction of the campaign, he nevertheless wanted to be near the front line to oversee the operation as it unfolded. Consequently, Hitler's personal train – codenamed 'Amerika' – was adapted as an improvised headquarters. This expedient was considered acceptable because, with the Soviet Union no longer a threat[1], the planners anticipated that the fighting in Poland would be over relatively quickly. Moreover, Führersonderzug (literally 'Führer Special Train')

[1] Following the German–Soviet Treaty of Non Aggression of August 1939.

'Amerika' had the advantage of flexibility; in the unlikely event that the western democracies came to the aid of their ally, the train would enable Hitler to shuttle between fronts.

During the war Hitler stayed in a number of purpose-built headquarters. The chart shows which *Führerhauptquartiere* Hitler occupied, when and for how long. (Author)

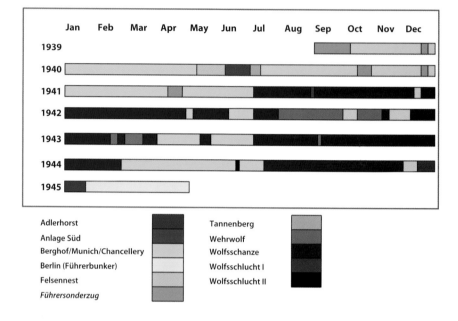

Today the *Führerhauptquartier* codenamed Felsennest has become overgrown with trees and bushes, but it is still possible to visit the remains. Just in front of the tree line shown there is a track that runs from Waldstrasse in the village of Rodert to the various destroyed bunkers. (Author)

A ANLAGE SÜD – *FÜHRERSONDERZUG*

The Polish Campaign was overseen by Hitler, not from a permanent *Führerhauptquartier*, but from his specially adapted train, Führersonderzug 'Amerika'. It was not ideally suited to the job but did give Hitler the flexibility he required to relocate his headquarters should Britain and France attack Germany from the west. In the end no concerted attack was launched by the western democracies and their caution was punished by a crushing defeat in May 1940. With his western flank secure, at least in the short term, Hitler now turned his attention east and once again the train served as an improvised headquarters for the Balkan campaign in

April 1941. Thereafter Hitler used specially constructed headquarters complexes, and the *Führersonderzug* was simply used to travel around the Reich.

One such excursion was made to FHQ Anlage Süd to meet his Italian ally Benito Mussolini in August 1941. Anlage Süd consisted of two separate facilities for accommodating trains that provided protection against air attack. At Strzyżów a rail tunnel had been adapted for the purpose and a short distance away at Stepina – and depicted in the artwork – a specially constructed concrete shelter had been built that was capable of accommodating the *Führersonderzug*.

Somewhat surprisingly, for Hitler at least, Britain and France honoured their pledge to protect Poland, but their attacks in the west were so ineffectual that they were little more than a minor irritation for the Wehrmacht, which was able to concentrate all of its might against Poland, and on 27 September the government in Warsaw capitulated. This favourable turn of events enabled Hitler and the Oberkommando der Wehrmacht (OKW) – the Armed Forces High Command – to monitor the campaign from their mobile headquarters without any major alarms. However, the shortcomings of this 'wandering camp', as Warlimont dubbed it, were recognized and it was concluded that a permanent solution would be needed for any attack in the west, which Hitler hoped to launch late in 1939. Thus, in September, Erwin Rommel, Dr Fritz Todt and Albert Speer were sent to the western border to identify possible sites.

Three sites were shortlisted[2] and, because there was no time to build a bespoke headquarters, all of them were based on pre-existing, but very different, structures. One was near Bad Münstereifel in the Eifel Mountains, one near Bad Nauheim in the Taunus Mountains and one near Freudenstadt in the Black Forest. The headquarters favoured by Speer was in the Taunus Mountains, an area he had explored as a young man. It was based around Schloß Ziegenberg and was codenamed FHQ Adlerhorst (Eagle's Eyrie). However, in spite of all the work to renovate the castle, it was clear that it would not be ready for the invasion, but more significantly Hitler was not enamoured with it. Speer later recollected how Hitler, following a visit to the castle, concluded that 'It was too luxurious... not his style, too grand, "something for a horse-loving aristocrat". In wartime, he said, he as Führer must inspire the soldiers at the front with the Spartan simplicity of his daily life.'

Having served as a *Gefreiter* with the List Regiment in World War I, Hitler was familiar with the privations of the humble soldier. He was also well aware of the value of concrete bunkers to protect against heavy artillery and, on the modern battlefield, air attack. With this in mind, Hitler chose FHQ Felsennest or 'Mountain Nest' – part of a flak position in the Westwall. Located in the Eifel it was in an ideal position for Hitler to oversee the campaign in the west and on 9 May 1940 Hitler and his staff moved in.

However, the rapid advance of the German forces in the spring of 1940 soon left Hitler somewhat detached in his hilltop bunker and he insisted that a new site be identified from where he could oversee the second phase of the attack. Once again there was no time to build a bespoke headquarters, so various other alternatives were considered. Dr Todt, together with members of the Führer Begleit Bataillon (Führer Escort Battalion), inspected a series of Maginot Line bunkers in the vicinity of Maubeuge, but this idea was quickly dismissed and a second reconnaissance mission was instigated, which identified a number of small villages that were considered suitable for adaptation. Of these Brûly-de-Pesche in Belgium was selected. A series of temporary and permanent buildings were erected in the village and existing buildings were modified to create what became known as FHQ Wolfsschlucht (Wolf's Gorge). Yet no sooner had Hitler moved in than approval was given to identify a site for a further *Führerhauptquartier* from where he could oversee operations deep inside France. North of Margival, between Reims and Soissons, was a railway tunnel that was considered suitable to house the

---

[2] Construction of an additional FHQ – Waldwiese (Forest Meadow) – began in October 1939 at Glan-Münchweiler. It was completed in April 1940, but was never used by Hitler.

Führersonderzug. Dr Todt and Oberstleutnant Thomas (the new Head of Security) surveyed the site and orders were given for the construction of a bunker ready for Hitler's use. Work on FHQ Wolfsschlucht II began on 15 June 1940, but two days later France sought an armistice and the plans were shelved.

With the threat in the west all but extinguished, Hitler's gaze once again turned east. Plans were now finalized for the invasion of the Soviet Union, but in the spring of 1941 Hitler was obliged to come to the aid of his Italian ally, Mussolini, whose forces had become mired in the Balkans. German troops were directed to help and Hitler once again utilized his personal train as an improvised headquarters. The forces of Yugoslavia, Greece and Albania, together with the supporting British and Commonwealth troops, were soon defeated, and Hitler could at last concentrate on the main prize – Stalin's Russia.

Hitler's view of the Soviet Union was contemptuous, insisting that 'We have only to kick in the door and the whole rotten edifice will come crashing down'. But his outward disdain masked a genuine fear that the Red Army, in spite of its shortcomings, was capable of delivering a powerful counter-strike. Thus, in late 1940 Hitler ordered Dr Todt and two of his adjutants, Schmundt and Engel, to identify three locations from where it would be possible to oversee operations against the Soviet Union. One of the sites was to be in East Prussia and would be the principal *Führerhauptquartier*, with two further smaller, less elaborate, sites in German-occupied Poland. The logic being that should the Red Army launch a counter-attack – particularly from the Bialystok salient – and threaten the main *Führerhauptquartier*, then Hitler could move to an alternative and oversee operations from there. These three headquarters – FHQ Wolfsschanze[3] at Rastenburg in East Prussia, Askania Mitte near Tomaszów and Askania Süd near Strzyzów (better known as Anlage Mitte and Anlage Süd) – were unique at the time because they were specially constructed to act as *Führerhauptquartiere*.

As it transpired, Hitler's concerns about a Soviet counter-attack proved groundless and although the Russian troops fought tenaciously, they were poorly led and were unable to stem the German advance. Consequently, Anlage Mitte was not used and Anlage Süd served only as a venue for talks with Mussolini in August 1941.

In that same summer German forces forged east and, as in France, the swift advance left Hitler far to the rear and unable to direct operations personally. Therefore, in September 1941, Thomas, Schmundt and Oberstleutnant Below (another of Hitler's adjutants) were ordered to identify three further sites for *Führerhauptquartiere* broadly corresponding to the axis of advance of the three German army groups: one in the north near Leningrad, one in the centre for the attack on Moscow and one in the Ukraine so that Hitler could direct operations in the Caucasus.

In October 1941 the OT was ordered to begin work at a former Red Army base near Gniesdovo, west of Smolensk, which lay on the main road to Moscow. Work on FHQ Bärenhöhle, as it was called, involved converting existing structures and building a number of new blockhouses. However,

---

[3] Initially codenamed 'Askania Nord', Hitler renamed it during the train journey to Rastenburg in June 1941. When Christa Schroeder, one of his secretaries, asked 'Why "Wolf" again, just like all the other HQs?' Hitler replied, 'That was my code name in the Years of Struggle'.
D. Irving, *Hitler's War and The War Path* (Focal Point Publications: London, 2002) p. 408.

From 1939 until the war's end Hitler's *Führerhauptquartier* programme consumed over 1 million cubic metres of concrete. The pie chart shows that more than half of the concrete was used at just two sites. (Author)

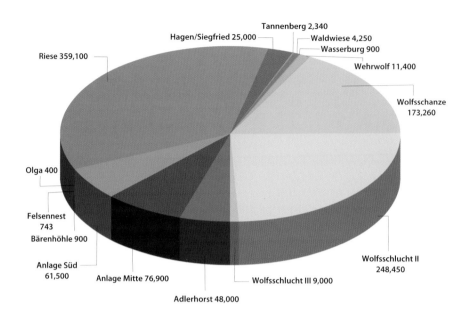

Tannenberg 2,340
Hagen/Siegfried 25,000
Waldwiese 4,250
Wasserburg 900
Riese 359,100
Wehrwolf 11,400
Wolfsschanze 173,260
Olga 400
Felsennest 743
Bärenhöhle 900
Anlage Süd 61,500
Anlage Mitte 76,900
Wolfsschlucht III 9,000
Wolfsschlucht II 248,450
Adlerhorst 48,000

although keen to capture the Soviet capital, Hitler's focus was increasingly fixed on the south and the vast natural resources located there. To better enable him to oversee operations in this theatre, orders were given for a second *Führerhauptquartier* to be built on Soviet territory. In November 1941 work began on Anlage Eichenhain (Camp Oak Grove) later renamed FHQ Wehrwolf[4]. The new *Führerhauptquartier* was located in a wood some 8km north of Vinnitsa in the Ukraine.

By the summer of 1942 work on these two *Führerhauptquartiere* was nearing completion ready for Hitler to take up residence and oversee the new offensive. The main effort was to be made in the south, with holding operations around Moscow and Leningrad. The latter had been blockaded by Axis forces since July 1941, but although symbolically important its capture

Brûly-de-Pesche today. To the right is the hotel – the *Wolfspalast* – in 1940. In the middle is the vicarage and to the left is the school. Just visible in the distance is the church steeple. Behind the trees to the left are the latrines and just out of view on the left was the village pump – still there but no longer functioning. (Author)

[4] In naming the new FHQ Hitler continued the wolf theme, but subtly altered the word 'werewolf' to 'wehrwolf' – 'wehr' being German for 'defence'.

was not a priority and troops were gradually redeployed to more important sections of the front. Consequently, it was not until November 1942 that work began on FHQ Wasserburg some 300km south-west of Leningrad. From here Hitler would oversee the capture of Russia's second city, but as it transpired he never visited the headquarters and in the summer of 1943 Axis forces around the city went on the defensive. Elsewhere offensive operations continued, as did the building of a new *Führerhauptquartier*. In July 1943 work began on FHQ Olga, to the north of Minsk. Some 400m³ of concrete were poured, but it was never completed.

Meanwhile, in the west, British and Commonwealth forces launched a series of raids against German-occupied Europe and forced Hitler to start fortifying the coast against further attacks. More significantly, following

ABOVE LEFT
The largest bunker at Wolfsschlucht II housed the staff department (and possibly the telephone exchange). The concrete bunker is just visible above the top of the outer building. (Author)

ABOVE
The concrete rail tunnel at Stepina was almost 500m long. Along its length entrances secured with steel doors were built into the wall to allow access. These could be secured from the inside with a simple locking mechanism. (Author)

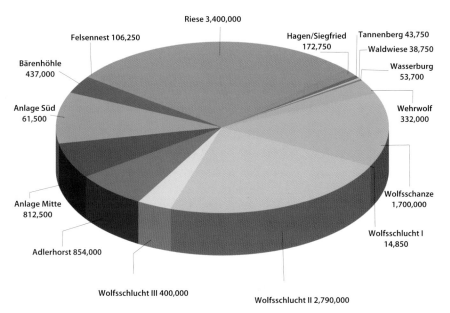

Riese 3,400,000
Felsennest 106,250
Hagen/Siegfried 172,750
Tannenberg 43,750
Waldwiese 38,750
Bärenhöhle 437,000
Wasserburg 53,700
Anlage Süd 61,500
Wehrwolf 332,000
Anlage Mitte 812,500
Wolfsschanze 1,700,000
Adlerhorst 854,000
Wolfsschlucht I 14,850
Wolfsschlucht III 400,000
Wolfsschlucht II 2,790,000

During the course of the war nearly 12 million working days were spent by the OT and other forced labourers constructing Hitler's various *Führerhauptquartiere*. The pie chart shows that ⅔ of the effort was expended on just three sites. (Author)

Hitler's decision to declare war on the United States there was an increasing threat of a full-scale invasion. To prepare for such an eventuality, work began on FHQ Wolfsschlucht III near Vendôme in May 1942, and soon after (September 1942) work resumed on the *Führerhauptquartier* at Margival. By the spring of 1944 the threat of invasion was acute and would, it was believed, be delivered in the region around Calais. If successful, such a landing would endanger the *Führerhauptquartiere* in France and so in April 1944 work began near Diedenhofen (Thionville) in Lorraine on FHQ Brunhilde[5], and in the autumn work was started at the Ohrdruf training ground in Thuringia.

Aside from the opening of a second front, Hitler's other great fear was Allied bombing. His secretary Traudl Junge recollected that in the spring of 1944, 'Hitler spoke more and more often of the possibility of a massive air raid on Führer headquarters. "They know exactly where we are, and some time they're going to destroy everything here with carefully aimed bombs. I expect them to attack any day," he said'. To counter this threat, further work was undertaken to strengthen the bunkers at FHQ Wolfsschanze. Whilst this work was going on Hitler headed to Berchtesgaden, which was itself being adapted to meet the threat of potentially devastating air attacks. As Hitler vacated Wolfsschanze for Bavaria in February 1944 he joked that 'We have built headquarters in just about every other corner of the Reich, but never dreamed we should one day need one near Italy!'

By the spring of 1944 FHQ Wolfsschanze was not only threatened from the air, it was also threatened by Red Army ground forces. To mitigate this risk, work began in October 1943 on a further site near Bad Charlottenbrunn (Jedlina-Zdrój) in Silesia. This was in a more central position and was therefore easier to defend and less threatened from the air. Führerhauptquartier Riese was incredibly resource intensive with manpower from the OT, forced labour from the nearby Gross Rosen concentration camp and later Poles captured in the Warsaw uprising working on the project. In October 1944, 23,000 workers were employed on the building work. The *Führerhauptquartier* was also a logistical nightmare requiring the transportation of tons of raw materials into this mountainous region and the removal of similar amounts of spoil. Below visited the site twice during the war and despaired at this 'superfluous' project that 'required huge quantities of cement and steel which were urgently required elsewhere.' Indeed, he was so concerned that he asked Speer if it could be stopped, but was told that would be impossible. Unsurprisingly FHQ Riese was never finished and in the closing stages of the war Hitler was instead forced to use *Führerhauptquartiere* from an earlier era or to improvise.

For the ill-fated Ardennes offensive Hitler stayed at FHQ Adlerhorst, though not in the palatial Schloß Ziegenberg – that was given over to Oberbefehlshaber West (OB West) Generalfeldmarschall Rundstedt and his staff. Hitler stayed in a series of bunkers at the rear of the castle. When Operation *Wacht am Rhein* (Watch on the Rhine) failed, Hitler was forced to return to Berlin where he retreated to a series of bunkers located under key government buildings in the heart of the city. Work on the first of these shelters began soon after Hitler became chancellor in 1933. Later, in 1936, he insisted that an air-raid shelter be included in the design for the banqueting hall in the garden behind the Reich Chancellery. Then, in 1942, perhaps anticipating the devastating air raids to come, Hitler asked Speer to develop

---

[5] In March 1943 work also began on FHQ Hagen (Siegfried) at Pullach, near Munich. However, Hitler and his advisors were seemingly unaware of the development.

plans for a much deeper and stronger bunker under the Reich Chancellery, but only in 1943 did work begin. The new shelter, known as the Führerbunker, became Hitler's last *Führerhauptquartier*, but even by the time of his suicide in April 1945 the work was incomplete.

THE PRINCIPLES OF COMMAND

Typically in the Osprey Fortress series this section would consider how the fortification in question was meant to work as a defensive position. Clearly such analysis would be of limited value in a discussion about Hitler's headquarters, because although they were defended, in the strictest sense of the word, they had no tactical value either defensively or offensively. Instead they acted as the nerve centre for the German high command and were where strategic and, increasingly, operational decisions about the direction of the war were made. To fully understand how and why the *Führerhauptquartiere* became the focus of military and political power in Germany in the war it is necessary to understand the power structure in Germany and in particular Hitler's leadership style.

Since the end of World War II historians have argued about Hitler's role and function within the Nazi system of rule. Some have contested that Hitler used his patronage intentionally as a tool to undermine any potential opposition through a strategy of 'divide and rule', while others have argued that his charismatic leadership style, the way the Nazis came to power, and the structure of the Nazi party, led to the creation of a fragmented system of government. What historians do not deny is that the government of Nazi Germany was chaotic and that Hitler's ability to act was necessarily limited by other power blocs, and yet, paradoxically, he was also the only source of real authority.

The fragmented nature of government was the result of a number of factors. Firstly, unlike in Russia, the Nazis' accession to power was by way of a bloodless coup; they did not overthrow the old elites, but rather colluded with them. As such, the power of big business and the military establishment was largely undiminished under the new regime, and in the development of policies and plans Hitler and the Nazis had to recognize their wishes.

The second factor was the Nazi Party itself. This was effectively a propaganda machine whose *raison d'être* was to win elections. However, although successful in its primary aim

Hitler, flanked by Stauffenberg, Puttkamer and Keitel (right) greets Bodenschatz in front of the guest bunker at Wolfsschanze on 15 July 1944. Of interest are the fake trees, which helped camouflage the headquarters from aerial observation. (Topfoto)

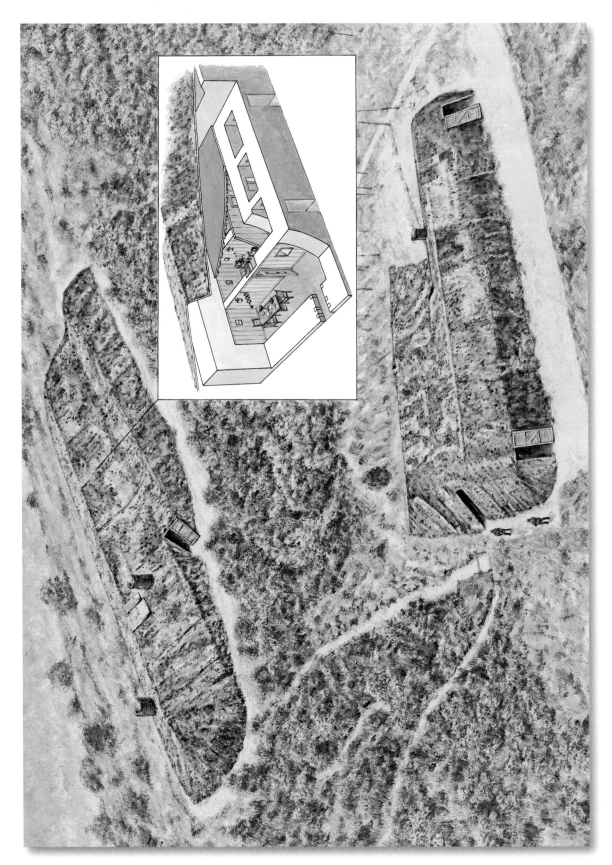

it was not structured to run a modern country like Germany and no attempt was made to adapt it so that it could be married with the state bureaucracy. Consequently, the party and state structures coexisted in an uneasy marriage.

Thirdly, Hitler's modus operandi was more about style than substance. Hitler rarely got involved in decision making, especially on domestic issues, where he considered his personal standing might suffer. As a result individuals and institutions filled the vacuum and rivalries flourished as they tried to outdo each other to curry favour with the Führer.

Yet while Hitler was happy to abrogate responsibility for domestic matters and the Jewish question, he was central to foreign policy (albeit often driven by military and economic pressures) and took the 'big' decisions – the remilitarization of the Rhineland and the *Anschluss* with Austria for example. The military, and in particular the Army, supported these actions, which were seen as simply reversing the unjust terms of the Paris Peace Settlement imposed on Germany at the end of World War I. Indeed, the military was broadly aligned with many Nazi policies including the introduction of conscription, increased military expenditure and the party's anti-Communist stance.

However, consensus on these issues could not disguise the underlying animosity that existed between the two groups, which was heightened by Hitler's increasingly belligerent foreign policy. The invasion of Poland brought with it war in Europe, as many in the military feared, but, tragically for those opposed to Hitler and his foreign policy, success in 1939 was followed by further victories in 1940. This convinced Hitler that he was a natural war leader like his illustrious predecessor and icon Frederick the Great. Believing that he was preordained for success, Hitler eschewed the idea of any high-level war committee and instead increasingly took to directing the war personally based on intuition and his experience of fighting in World War I. To do this he would need to be near the front and so he ordered the construction of a series of headquarters from where he could oversee operations, shuttling between them on his personal train.

Accommodation on the *Führersonderzug* and at the various headquarters was constrained by available space, and only members of Hitler's inner circle and senior OKW staff were catered for, but one imagines that even if space had not been an issue the Oberkommando des Heeres (OKH) staff would not have received an invite. That said, the feeling was undoubtedly mutual; many senior

B FELSENNEST, BAD MÜNSTEREIFEL

Hitler chose FHQ Felsennest as his headquarters for the planned invasion of France and the Low Countries in 1940. The facility was set into the hillside above the village of Rodert and lay within Luftverteidigungszone West – the anti-aircraft defence zone of the Westwall – and consisted of a series of bunkers and anti-aircraft emplacements constructed in 1938–39. Work to adapt the facility for its new role began in October 1939.

The main compound consisted of two bunkers and three barrack blocks, which were surrounded by a security fence and watchtowers and formed what was known as Sperrkreis I. The two bunkers were based on standard designs developed as part of the LVZ West. The larger bunker (a 'K Stand') was 16 x 8m and was constructed using 454m³ of reinforced concrete. It was capable of accommodating 24 men in five separate rooms, but was adapted so that half served as Hitler's study and bedroom

and the other half was used by his manservant Linge, his adjutant Schaub, as well as Keitel, Jodl and Schmundt. The bunker was provided with two external entrances, each covered by loopholes. These led into a gas-proof room which in turn led to the main corridor linking the rooms; Hitler's private rooms were to the left. Adjacent to the bunker was the officer's barrack block which also housed a teleprinter.

The smaller bunker (an 'F Stand') was 10.8 x 7.6m and was constructed from reinforced concrete, some 289m³ in total. Two separate doors, each again covered by internal loopholes, provided access to the facility. A gas lock protected the main living quarters – two rooms that were originally designed to take nine men, but which now served as a meeting room and air-raid shelter for the larger barrack block next door. This was home to the kitchen and a dining hall, which had a long table that could seat 20 people and was where all meals were taken.

Army officers disliked intensely the idea of a former Austrian *Gefreiter* directing operations.

Yet whilst the Army was happy to keep its distance from the Führer so that he wasn't scrutinizing every decision, Hitler's inner circle – Himmler, Göring and Ribbentrop – were keen to be as close as possible. The rationale for this can be traced back to Hitler's leadership style and his desire not to get involved in domestic issues, which led to the proliferation of a series of powerful fiefdoms (the OT, the SS, etc.) whose power relied on Hitler's patronage. This was especially true during the war when this 'inner circle' needed to be close to their patron to ensure they benefited from any carving up of the spoils of war. To that end, Himmler, Göring and Ribbentrop had a liaison officer at the *Führerhauptquartier* to keep them abreast of developments and each had his own train with which they used to follow Hitler around. However, attempts to be accommodated at Hitler's various headquarters were resisted and they had to make their own arrangements.

The one exception to this exclusion policy was Martin Bormann, who had his own bunker at FHQ Wolfsschanze and later his own house at FHQ Adlerhorst. This was significant, because, as O'Donnell notes: 'As Goebbels, Speer and others have observed, the isolation of the Führer was the making of Bormann. The cramped geography of bunkers was ideal for his slow takeover operation, and by 1943 Bormann controlled all access to Hitler except that of the high military.'

A TOUR OF THE SITES

Adlerhorst

Führerhauptquartier Adlerhorst was based around the imposing Schloß Ziegenberg, which had been compulsorily purchased at the outbreak of the war. No expense was spared in renovating the interior of the castle so that it was fit for a head of state; it was finished with walnut doors and window frames, had panelled walls and was furnished with paintings and sculptures. From the castle, steps led down to a series of subterranean concrete bunkers. The first of these, Bunker 1, was arranged like an old-style railway carriage with the various rooms (which included a map room, recreation room and toilets) accessed from a single corridor. A passageway led from here to four further bunkers. The first of these was Bunker 5, which housed the fuel tanks, ventilation system, machine room and generator, coal store and the heating and water boiler. From here the corridor continued to Bunkers 6 and 7. The former housed the telephone exchange (Amt 600) and the latter an accommodation block. The last bunker, Bunker 3, was adjacent to Bunker 1 and was an accommodation block consisting of some 16 rooms.

Some 2km north of the castle seven 'houses' were built, each with a reinforced concrete cellar. Where the cellar stood proud of the ground the walls were clad with natural stone and then on top a Swiss-style chalet was constructed, which provided the day-to-day accommodation for the residents. Haus I was designated as Hitler's quarters and included a map room, rooms for his aides-de-camp and servants and his own private quarters, which consisted of a bedroom, bathroom, dressing room and study. The cellar was reached by a flight of stairs and provided a pared-down version of the upstairs accommodation.

A roofed walkway led from Hitler's accommodation to Haus II – the officers' mess. This consisted of a large dining hall, two lounges and a kitchen.

Next to the mess or *Kasino* was Haus IV – the *Generalshaus* – which could accommodate 12 people in a mixture of single and double rooms and also had a lounge and two offices. Next to this was Haus III, the *Pressehaus* where Otto Dietrich and his staff worked, and finally there was Haus V, which was allotted to Martin Bormann. To the north of Hitler's house was Haus VI, which was home to the OKW staff and a telephone exchange. At the bottom of the rise on which the other six 'houses' sat, and separated by a small road, was Haus VII – the guardhouse. This was much larger than the others and was of a slightly different design, with a porch at one end and a garage at the other.

Anlage Mitte

Anlage Mitte was located east of Lodz near the town of Tomaszów and was split into three parts. The first, Anlage Mitte I, consisted of a 300m-long railway tunnel bored into the side of a mountain. A gallery leading off the main tunnel linked it to the machinery/pump house, which supplied fresh air, water and electricity. Outside the tunnel, a *Teehaus* (tea house) and huts to accommodate Hitler's personal retinue and security staff were erected. Beyond the tunnel a reinforced concrete 'tube' was constructed that was capable of housing Hitler's train. This was known as Anlage Mitte II. A gallery linked the tunnel to the machinery/pump house.

Anlage Mitte III consisted of a Type 102v *Doppelgruppenunterstand*. This was a standard bunker design used in the Westwall from 1939. It consisted of two rooms linked to the outside by two entrances, which were protected by a gas lock. In addition to the bunker there were two further concrete blockhouses, as well as six further wooden huts to accommodate OKH staff and security personnel.

Anlage Süd

Anlage Süd was split over two sites. At Strzyzów an existing railway tunnel that had been constructed by the Austrians before World War I was adapted to accommodate Hitler's train. Just outside the tunnel entrance a building to

One of the 'Type 102v' concrete shelters built near the rail tunnel at Stepina. This example was located adjacent to the tunnel and was fitted with two loopholes – one in each room and accessed through separate doors. (Author)

One of the three concrete pillboxes built around the tunnel at Stepina to protect the facility. Each pillbox was fitted with three apertures for machine guns. Access was through a single entrance sealed with a steel door, though, if necessary, an emergency exit was provided. (Author)

house pumps and generators was constructed and huts were provided for security staff, as a well as a *Teehaus* for Hitler.

A short distance to the north, at Frysztak, a reinforced concrete tunnel, similar to that at Anlage Mitte, was constructed. It was 7m high and almost 500m long, and was designed to house the *Führersonderzug*. It was serviced by a machinery/pump house and around the perimeter were located two large concrete shelters (Type 102v) and three pillboxes, each with three loopholes, which provided protection.

Bärenhöhle

Führerhauptquartier Bärenhöhle was located 9km west of Smolensk on the site of a former Red Army headquarters. Much of the infrastructure was reused or modified, but even so the OT and Russian labourers had to undertake a considerable amount of work to prepare it for its new role. A large reinforced concrete bunker was built for the Führer and more than 30 barrack blocks were erected to accommodate his staff; each was furnished with furniture and fittings 'liberated' from the Russians. The whole complex was enclosed by a perimeter fence almost 2km in length.

Water was supplied via two wells drilled 120m into the ground. Waste water was channelled to a sewage plant where it was treated and passed into the River Dnieper. Power was supplied from the civilian network, but diesel generators were installed to ensure continuity of supply should there be any disruption.

The train station at Gniesdovo was upgraded with the platform lengthened to accommodate the *Führersonderzug*.

Brunhilde

At Diedenhofen (Thionville) in Lorraine some 15,300m² of tunnels of the Maginot Line were restored for use as a *Führerhauptquartier* known as FHQ Brunhilde. These tunnels would accommodate not only the Führer but also Himmler and the OKH, and were navigated, in part, by means of a narrow-gauge railway. Above-ground wooden huts were erected and two

The bunkers at Felsennest, where Hitler oversaw the invasion of France and the Low Countries, were later demolished. The remnants are slowly being reclaimed by nature, but it is still possible to see details of the original structure. Here the imprint of the shuttering used in the pouring of the concrete is clearly visible. (Author)

bunkers were built – one of which was similar in design to the *Führerbunker* at Wolfsschlucht II.

Felsennest

Führerhauptquartier Felsennest was located in and around the village of Rodert, which lay in the so-called Luftverteidigungszone West of the Westwall. Sperrkreis I (Security Zone I) was located on a small wooded hill just to the south-west of the village. It consisted of a larger bunker with wood-clad walls and an adjoining hut. The bunker housed Hitler's study and bedroom and additionally was home to his personal staff Schaub and Linge as well as Generalfeldmarschall Keitel. Adjacent was another hut and a smaller bunker where Jodl, Hitler's three adjutants, Keitel's aide-de-camp and Dr Brandt were

On around 6 March 1945 retreating German troops demolished the bunkers at FHQ Felsennest. Here, soldiers of the First US Army inspect the remains. The scale of the structure is clear from the GI standing amongst the rubble. (US National Archives)

accommodated. A little distance away was a further hut where situation conferences were held. The whole of Sperrkreis I was surrounded by a fence with security towers. The village and surrounding countryside, some 30 hectares in total, was designated Sperrkreis II. A number of buildings in the village were commandeered by the WFSt and were adapted for their use; these included offices, facilities for guests, a kitchen, garage and various air-raid shelters.

Führerbunker (Berlin)

The bunkers that were constructed beneath the Reich Chancellery were originally designed as air-raid shelters, but the incessant bombing forced Hitler and his staff to seek permanent refuge underground and these rooms were adapted for use as an improvised *Führerhauptquartier*. The so-called *Vorbunker*, from the earliest build phase, consisted of 12 rooms branching off a single corridor. In the final act of the war, a number of the rooms were given over to Goebbels and his family with the rest used to store, prepare, cook and serve food for the residents. From the *Vorbunker* a set of stairs led down to the Führerbunker. This was not only deeper underground, but also a significantly stronger construction with a roof almost 3m thick and walls over 2m thick. An armoured door protected the main access to the bunker. Beyond this were 20 or so small rooms reached by a long corridor. On the right of this corridor were a series of rooms that housed the engine room, ventilation equipment and the small telephone switchboard. It was also home to the medical room and a separate cabin for Hitler's personal physician. Farther down the main corridor, on the left, were Hitler's private rooms. The section of corridor that led to his apartments served as a waiting room and, by contrast with the rest of the bunker, was lavishly decorated with red carpet and paintings rescued from the Chancellery. From the corridor a small ante-room led to Hitler's study, which was furnished with a sofa, a radio and a desk, above which was a picture of Frederick the Great. A door led to Hitler's bedroom. This was again sparsely furnished with a bed, a safe and an oxygen cylinder. A further door led from Hitler's study to his dressing room and Eva Braun's bedroom/sitting room. Next to the ante-room was the cramped conference room where all the military briefings were held. At the end of the main corridor was a cloakroom and finally an exit with a flight of stairs that led out into the Chancellery garden.

Hagen

Führerhauptquartier Hagen (Siegfried) was located near the village of Pullach, south of Munich. It was built on an estate that housed Party functionaries and fell under the auspices of Martin Bormann. The *Führerhauptquartier* (which Hitler seemingly did not know about) consisted of seven wooden huts for accommodation and a further four huts, the roofs, walls and windows of which had been strengthened so that they provided protection against shell and bomb splinters. Two railway sidings that were linked to the main line via a branch line were constructed so that two *Sonderzüge* (special trains) could be accommodated.

A bunker for Hitler and his staff was built underground and was 70m long by 20m wide and approximately 11m high with a 3m-thick roof. It consisted of some 30 rooms, including work and conference rooms as well as rooms for the ventilation system, machinery, transformers and switches. Access was via a tower, which was fitted with both a lift and stairs. At the opposite end of the bunker a further flight of stairs formed an emergency exit.

Olga

Some 200km north-east of Minsk, near the village of Orsha, was FHQ Olga. There were plans to build a series of bunkers and huts here, but when the site was abandoned the *Führerbunker* had not been completed.

Riese

In November 1943 work began on FHQ Riese. The site chosen was south-east of Bad Charlottenbrunn in a mountainous and heavily forested area of Lower Silesia. Rather than a single location, Riese consisted of a series of underground facilities that were bored by specialist engineers. The exposed rock face was then sealed with concrete and faced with stone. The entrances were protected with armoured doors against bomb blasts. When completed, the tunnels would be capable of accommodating more than 20,000 staff including Hitler and his retinue, security personnel as well as heads of the Army, Luftwaffe and the SS along with their staffs and the Reich foreign minister.

While work continued on the underground tunnels, in 1944 the nearby Schloß Fürstenstein was commandeered by the OT. Work started immediately on transforming it into a residence for Ribbentrop and his staff, with room also set aside for the Führer. From the castle, access was made to underground galleries that could be used in an air raid. It was also planned to have a bomb-proof siding for the *Führersonderzug*. When the war ended, the work at Riese, though extensive, was far from complete.

Tannenberg

Führerhauptquartier Tannenberg (Pine Mountain) was located between Baden-Baden and Freudenstadt on a 1,000m-high feature in the heart of the Black Forest called the Kniebis. The site was just off the Black Forest High Road and was on the site of an existing installation of the Luftverteidigungszone West. Two bunkers were constructed; one was for Hitler's use and the other, south of the road, was a *Nachrichtenbunker* (communication centre). In addition a series of wooden barrack blocks were built, one to accommodate Hitler and a further one to house Keitel and Jodl. There was also an officers' mess, a *Teehaus*, a hut for situation conferences (*Lagehaus*), barracks for *Führerhauptquartier* staff and security personnel, a guardhouse and a shower block. The whole of Sperrkreis I was protected by a barbed-wire fence. Unusually, Warlimont's OKW staff stayed in a local guesthouse a kilometre away.

Waldwiese

Führerhauptquartier Waldwiese was built around the village of Glan-Münchweiler, near Landstuhl, and consisted of a series of bunkers and huts. The *Führerbunker* was constructed in woodland to the east of the village, while a communications bunker was built in the

As the tide of the war turned German forces were pushed back towards the borders of Germany and forward headquarters constructed for Hitler had to be demolished so that they did not fall into enemy hands. Here are some of the remains of FHQ Wehrwolf, which can still be seen in Ukraine today. (Topfoto)

village itself and was camouflaged with a slate roof and painted windows so that it looked like a normal dwelling.

Wasserburg

Führerhauptquartier Wasserburg was situated near Pskov on the River Welikaya and, like FHQ Adlerhorst, was based around a large mansion that was renovated to accommodate Hitler and his staff, including an officers' mess that was located in the mansion's central tower. Outbuildings were also adapted as accommodation and some of the Reichsarbeitsdienst (RAD) huts were used as quarters for security personnel. Outside the mansion a standard Type 102v bunker was constructed for Hitler's use in the event of an air raid. A specially designed garage was also built, which was heated so that vehicle engines would start even in the hardest of winters.

Electricity was provided to the site from the power station at Pskov, which was stepped down through a newly built transformer. From here overhead cables connected the various buildings. Water was supplied to the headquarters from a natural spring, and was pumped into a large header tank that fed individual standpipes. A separate tank stored water to serve the system

Before the Germans departed, FHQ Wehrwolf was demolished. Large sections of concrete still remain at the site; this piece is complete with ventilation grill. (E. Hitriak and I. Volkov)

C   WEHRWOLF, VINNITSA

As German forces drove deeper into the Soviet Union, Hitler's eastern headquarters, FHQ Wolfsschanze near Rastenburg in East Prussia, became increasingly distant from the main focus of events. As a result new sites for potential *Führerhauptquartiere* were reconnoitred and three sites were identified – one to the north near Pskov (FHQ Wasserburg), from where Hitler would oversee any further attack on Leningrad; one in the centre near Smolensk (FHQ Bärenhöhle), from where he could direct operations against the Soviet capital and one to the south near Vinnitsa (FHQ Wehrwolf) from where Hitler could oversee any thrust into the Caucasus. Only the last of these headquarters was used by the Führer.

Hitler was resident at FHQ Wehrwolf from July until November 1942. Soon thereafter the Red Army launched its powerful counter-attack at Stalingrad and encircled Paulus' Sixth Army. Hitler plotted its relief from FHQ Wolfsschanze and did not return to FHQ Wehrwolf until February 1943, where he watched Manstein's masterful counter-stroke in the Donets Basin unfold. Following a final visit in August, his headquarters was taken over by Army Group South, but this proved to be only temporary and eventually FHQ Wehrwolf had to be abandoned.

In December 1943 the buildings were demolished; the remnants of the concrete bunkers are still visible.

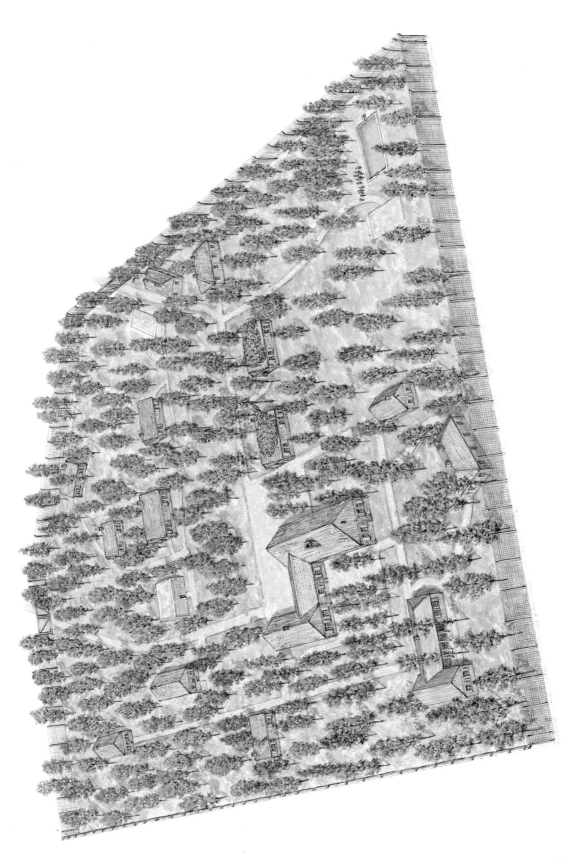

of fire hydrants. Waste water was channelled to the newly constructed sewage-treatment facilities. From here the treated water was pumped into the river.

The access road to the site was resurfaced and around the facility 1,800m of 'Flanders hedge' was erected.

Wehrwolf

In November 1941 work began on FHQ Wehrwolf, which was located in woodland just off the main route to Shitomir and 8km north of Vinnitsa. The facility consisted of a number of bunkers, blockhouses and huts all constructed by the OT.

Sperrkreis I, where Hitler was housed, was located at the far end of the clearing where, according to Baur, 'Two bunkers were built, one for Hitler and his essential staff, the other for the rest of the workers on the base. They were planned only for protection in the event of bombings'. However, for day-to-day use Hitler and his staff were accommodated in 19 blockhouses constructed, at Hitler's behest, from non-treated timber, as on previous occasions Hitler had been badly affected by the fumes from the wood preservatives.

Water was supplied to the headquarters from two wells and was used for drinking and for more general use, including the filling of the swimming pool that had been specially built. Water for the fire hydrants was pumped from the River Bug, and this is also where the effluent from the sewage plant was pumped.

Hitler spent a considerable amount of time at Wehrwolf and it soon became clear that more room was needed, so in January 1943 work began on a second building phase that saw the construction of further blockhouses, huts, roads and paths. It also necessitated lengthening the perimeter fences from 6km to 7.6km.

The site was extensively camouflaged with nets threaded with sea grass, and vegetation from the forest was also used. Some of the larger trees around the edge of the forest were adapted to serve as lookout towers, and, unusually, underground guard posts were dug for Hitler's security personnel.

Wolfsschanze

Führerhauptquartier Wolfsschanze was built in the Görlitz Forest in East Prussia. It straddled the road from Rastenburg (Ketrzyn) to Angerburg (Wegorzewo) and the rail line that ran broadly parallel. Work on the site was almost continuous from when the first sod was cut in 1940 to when Hitler left for the last time in November 1944, but was essentially divided into three phases: 1940–41, 1942–43 and 1944.

Phase 1

This consisted of concrete and brick hutments with steel shutters to protect the windows and included, in Sperrkreis I, accommodation for Hitler and his personal staff, Bormann, Keitel and security personnel as well as a mess, communication centre, garage and heating plant. In addition, there were a number of wooden buildings, including a *Teehaus*, which Hitler used as a place of relaxation.

Phase 2

As the war dragged on it was realized that the accommodation would need to be extended. Initially wooden hutments were built, but later these were strengthened with the addition of concrete roofs and brick walls. Much of this

accommodation was functional in purpose with offices for Jodl and Göring, but also recreational buildings including guest accommodation, a second mess, a new *Teehaus*, a sauna and a cinema. Wooden annexes were also added to Keitel and Hitler's bunker – the latter being used as a study.

Outside of Sperrkreis I, south of the road, accommodation was provided for Kriegsmarine, Luftwaffe, foreign ministry, OT and SS liaison officers and their respective staffs.

Phase 3

In the final building phase, which began in February 1944, a number of key buildings were massively strengthened including Hitler's, Keitel's and Bormann's bunkers, the communication bunkers in both Sperrkreis I and II and the guest bunker. There was also a new bunker for Göring, a new general-purpose bunker adjacent to Bormann's and two further bunkers south of the road that were to be used by staff as an air-raid shelter.

Hitler had sketched out the design for the new bunker himself and wanted the existing structure encased in 3m-thick concrete. Then he wanted a further concrete jacket, some 5m thick, and in between the two he wanted a layer of sand that would serve to absorb any bomb blast. According to Speer, when complete 'It looked like an ancient Egyptian tomb. It was actually nothing but a great windowless block of concrete, without direct ventilation, in cross section a building whose masses of concrete far exceeded the usable cubic feet of space'. He concluded his appraisal by noting that: 'It seemed as if the concrete walls sixteen and a half feet thick that surrounded Hitler separated him from the outside world in a figurative as well as literal sense, and locked him up inside his delusions.'

At the outset, work on the headquarters was undertaken in the utmost secrecy with the plans for the site initially referred to as a chemical works. Great efforts were expended on camouflaging the site with netting and fake trees and bushes located on the roofs. The *Führersonderzug*, when kept at

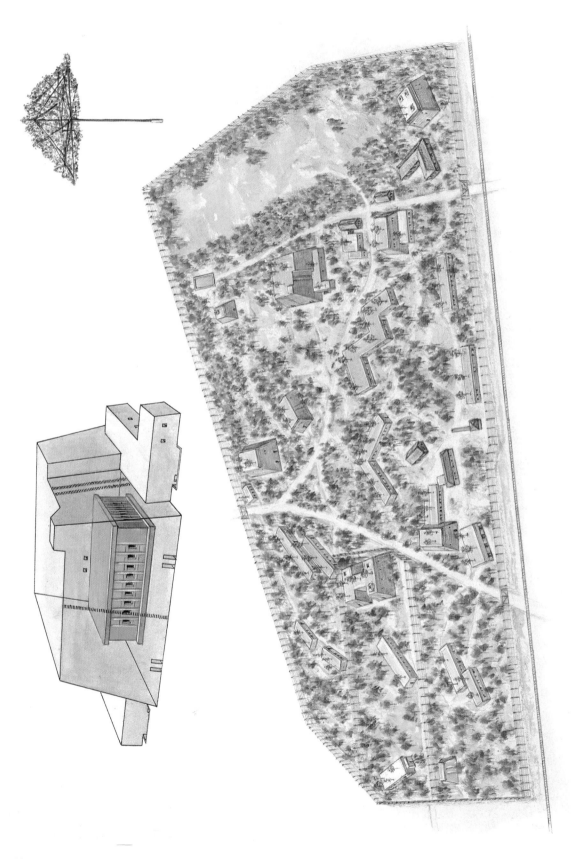

Görlitz, was also camouflaged. Aerial photographs were taken to ensure that the camouflage was effective. The road and the train line through the site were closed to the public, as was the small station of Görlitz, which was now expanded so that it could accommodate the *Führersonderzug* and the trains of other visiting dignitaries.

The site itself was divided into a series of security zones. Sperrkreis I was located at the eastern end of the complex and was fenced with two entrances, one to the east and one to the west. This inner security zone was the nerve centre of Wolfsschanze and was where Hitler and his inner circle (Bormann, Göring and Keitel) were accommodated. Ultimately it also included accommodation for Jodl and the WFSt staff, messes, accommodation for guests, Hitler's personal staff, security guards and liaison staff. It also had garages and a communication bunker, and was the location for the typists' office, which had its own fence to ensure the sensitive material processed there was not compromised.

In September 1943 a further security zone – Sperrkreis A – was established. A fence was constructed around the *Führerbunker* and the buildings in the immediate vicinity. Access to the area was closely controlled. Later, when Hitler's bunker was being strengthened, another security zone was established around the guest bunker where Hitler resided temporarily and an adjacent building – the *Lagebaracke* – and it was here that the unsuccessful July plot was perpetrated (see Plate H).

A further security zone for Warlimont's WFSt and headquarters commandant staff was constructed to the south-west of Sperrkreis I. The accommodation consisted of single-storey concrete and brick houses, but in 1944 was supplemented with an enormous *Nachrichtenbunker* to protect the telephone exchange. Adjacent to this and south of Sperrkreis I were buildings to accommodate OKM and OKL liaison officers and Ribbentrop's staff.

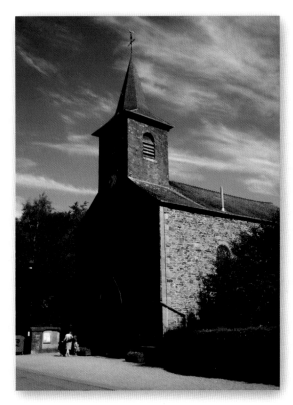

The Church of Sainte Meér at Brûly-de-Pesche as it is today. In 1940 the upper section of the spire was removed to make it less conspicuous and the building itself was used by the OT. The Church has since been returned to its former use and is still used for worship. (Author)

A modern view of the *Wolfspalast* at Brûly-de-Pesche. In the war the building was used as a signals centre and to accommodate *Führerhauptquartier* staff. Afterwards the former inn was turned into a hotel with the addition of a terrace at the front. (Author)

The entire site was surrounded by a further fence and was known as Sperrkreis II. It had three entrances: in the west, the east and the south – the latter linked the headquarters with the airfield at Rastenburg 6km distant. The entrances were guarded and further blockhouses and machine-gun posts were located around the perimeter along with flak positions to guard against air attack. Extensive use was made of minefields and farther afield strategic road junctions were guarded.

Wolfsschlucht I

Wolfsschlucht I was based around the Belgian village of Brûly-de-Pesche. It consisted of six buildings, which were modified for their new role. The OT began work on 25 May 1940 with the vicarage, the village inn (renamed the *Wolfspalast*) and the school being converted into accommodation for Keitel, guest accommodation and an operations room respectively. The church tower was removed to disguise the structure and was 'put in a safe place' to be rebuilt again when the fighting was over. The main body of the church was used for offices and the nave partitioned off and used as a small cinema.

In addition to the conversion work a series of concrete bunkers and wooden buildings were constructed. In the forest a wooden chalet was built for Hitler, along with a *Teehaus* and a further wooden barrack block to house the OKW command staff (WFSt Section L). A small bunker (25m²) was also built as an air-raid shelter. This could be accessed from either side and was fitted with steel gas-proof doors. A further bunker was planned near the *Wolfspalast* but was not completed. Next to it was a short aircraft landing strip. The garrison headquarters was located in a house on the road leading into the village. The whole site was secured with barbed wire.

Wolfsschlucht II

Wolfsschlucht II was constructed at the entrance to a rail tunnel between the villages of Neuville-sur-Margival and Laffaux; the idea being that the *Führersonderzug* could be safely parked in the tunnel, which had been fitted with armoured doors at the entrance, to protect against air attack.

The compound itself comprised of six large bunkers and a mixture of other buildings, some of them with strengthened walls, roofs and windows. The

Führerbunker consisted of a reinforced concrete air-raid shelter with walls some 3.5m thick, which was surrounded on two sides by an outer building that consisted of work rooms, a hall, kitchen, WCs and bath and shower rooms.

Adjacent to the *Führerbunker* was the OKW bunker, which was similar in set-up with a massive air-raid shelter surrounded on three sides by an outer building consisting of more than 20 rooms and a further annexe with almost as many rooms again. Finally, in this group was the largest of the buildings, which served as the staff department with offices, living quarters and a telephone exchange. In construction it followed the same format as the others, with outbuildings on three sides of a reinforced concrete bunker which was itself divided into four sections.

On the other side of the railway line was a smaller signals bunker with teleprinter and annexe. Farther down the railway line towards Margival was a guest bunker that was not dissimilar to the staff department bunker, but was divided into three sections. Finally there was a further bunker, which was on the opposite side of the track from Margival station. Internally this was divided into two and a garage was attached.

The main *Führerhauptquartier* buildings were surrounded by a belt of some 450 other positions, many of them anti-aircraft emplacements to accommodate heavy, medium and light anti-aircraft guns, rangefinders and searchlights.

Wolfsschlucht III

Although Hitler had ordered that only one *Führerhauptquartier* was necessary in France, a further facility was constructed 15km west of Vendôme. Once again it was built around a railway tunnel that was fitted with armoured doors to protect the *Führersonderzug*. At the north-east tunnel entrance a bunker was constructed for Hitler and another one for his staff. As was the case at Wolfsschlucht II, a series of anti-aircraft emplacements were built to protect against air attack.

Führersonderzug

As the head of state, Hitler was entitled to use special trains provided by the Reichsbahn (German Railways). However, starting in 1937 Hitler ordered the construction of a series of new armoured coaches that were to be for his

The OKW bunker at Wolfsschlucht II was later renamed 'Zucarello'. The road in front leads to the *Teehaus*. Hitler's bunker is to the right, out of the shot. (Author)

Wolfsschlucht II was protected from air attack by a series of flak batteries. This position on the road between Margival and Laffaux was designed to take a light or medium anti-aircraft gun. The niches at the side were for ammunition. (Author)

E WOLFSSCHLUCHT, BRÛLY-DE-PESCHE

Hitler oversaw the second stage of the western campaign (Operation *Rot*, or red), which commenced on 5 June 1940, from the small Belgian village of Brûly-de-Pesche. The village consisted of six buildings and was perfect as a headquarters, nestling unobtrusively in the Fôret de Gondreux. Work to transform the sleepy fishing village (hence its name) began at the end of May. Men of the OT moved in and those residents who had not left in the face of the German advance were now evacuated.

The church of Sainte Meér became the headquarters for the OT and to make it less conspicuous the spire was removed (although later replaced). The vicarage next door became Keitel's headquarters, and the school and latrines were used as offices. The church was also later used as offices when building work was complete and the OT had departed. The village inn – renamed the '*Wolfspalast*' (Wolf's Palace) – was adapted to

accommodate staff and guests and just to the side a landing strip was prepared that was long enough for the versatile Fieseler Storch light aircraft to land. Behind the inn, on the road leading into the village, was the *Führerhauptquartier* commandant's office (not shown).

In addition to these alterations a series of new bunkers and temporary buildings were constructed. Close to the shrine to Sainte Meér in the nearby forest a chalet was built for Hitler (the *Führerwohnung*) along with a *Teehaus* and a concrete air-raid shelter. The latter was never used by the Führer – even during an actual raid. He preferred to be outside and away from the insects that infested the area. A further barrack block was built in the forest nearby to accommodate the OKW command staff. Surrounding the whole village was a barbed-wire fence.

personal use only. These were completed by August 1939 and the special train was codenamed 'Amerika'[6]. It consisted of a locomotive, two baggage cars (one at each end) and 11 carriages, painted dark green. The first of these was the Führer's Pullman carriage (No. 10206) – the '*Führerwagen*' – which consisted of a series of compartments: two for Hitler, including a bathroom, and others for his personal staff to sleep and wash in. This was followed by a *Befehlswagen* (command car), which was split in two. The forward half accommodated the conference room, including the map table, and the rear half housed the telephone exchange and signals centre. The third coach accommodated Hitler's personal bodyguards. There were then two dining carriages – one for the Führer and one for his staff, two sleeping carriages, a bathing carriage (with showers and hip baths), two carriages for Hitler's retinue (adjutants, personal physician, secretaries, cooks etc.) and a *Pressewagen* for Dietrich and his staff, which included a short-wave transmitter.

With the outbreak of the war the train was adapted for use as a mobile headquarters. Externally the main visible difference was the addition of two flak wagons, armed with 2cm Flakvierling 38s, one at the front between the locomotives and the first car and the other at the tail of the train. Later in the war the locomotives were armoured to protect against air attack.

THE LIVING SITE

Hitler's time at the various *Führerhauptquartiere* was spent in the company of a small circle of individuals. The more senior figures like Joseph Goebbels (propaganda minister), Hermann Göring (head of the Luftwaffe), Heinrich Himmler (head of the SS) and Joachim von Ribbentrop (Foreign Minister) only tended to visit, having their own accommodation. The one exception was Martin Bormann, Hitler's private secretary, who, like Hitler's staff, resided permanently with the Führer.

A number of Hitler's closest staff, like Julius Schaub, Hitler's chief personal adjutant, had been with him since the early days of the Nazi party. Other personal adjutants joined his staff later and included Albert Bormann (brother of Martin, but whose relationship was so strained that they only ever spoke through intermediaries) and Otto Günsche, who was with the Führer until the very end and ignited the petrol to incinerate his chief and his wife after they had committed suicide. He was assisted by Erich Kempka, Hitler's driver, who provided the petrol for the cremation and Heinz Linge, his valet, who helped carry Hitler's body from the bunker. Also in the bunker at the end was Hans Baur, Hitler's personal pilot.

Hitler's personal well being, wherever he travelled, was catered for by his personal physicians – Dr Theodor Morell and Dr Karl Brandt – although the former arguably did more to worsen Hitler's condition with the medicines he prescribed than he did to ameliorate them.

Hitler's meals were prepared at the *Führerhauptquartiere* by his personal cook, an Austrian by the name of Fraulein Manzialy. They were invariably simple dishes in keeping with Hitler's vegetarianism (although he did have a predilection – verging on an addiction in his final days – for cakes). His meals were invariably taken with his secretaries who seemed to give the Führer an opportunity to escape from talk of the war and discuss lighter subjects that

---

[6] Following Germany's declaration of war on America in December 1941, the name of the train was changed to 'Brandenburg'.

A view of the *Wolfspalast* at Brûly-de-Pesche. Just visible is the outline of what was the barn door. When the building formed part of the *Führerhauptquartier* the door was inscribed with the building's name. (Author)

eased his mood. During the course of the war Hitler had four secretaries – Gerda Christian (née Daranowski), Traudl Junge, Christa Schroeder and Johanna Wolf, the eldest of the group.

Hitler was also supported by numerous military advisers and liaison officers: Rudolf Schmundt (Chief Military Adjutant) and one adjutant for each of the armed services. These were Engel (Army), Below (Luftwaffe) and Puttkamer (Kriegsmarine). There were also three liaison officers: Bodenschatz (Luftwaffe), Karl Wolff (SS) and Admiral Voss. In addition, Hitler was advised by senior OKW officers who also travelled with him and were accommodated in the various *Führerhauptquartiere*. Principal among these were Generalfeldmarschall Wilhelm Keitel (head of the OKW), Generaloberst Jodl (Chief of the Operations Staff of the Armed Forces) and Jodl's deputy, General Walter Warlimont (head of the WFSt Land Defence Section).

These companions were with Hitler throughout the war and their lives in the various *Führerhauptquartiere* revolved around his schedule. This gradually changed and became increasingly bizarre as Hitler's physical and mental state deteriorated. However, it broadly followed the same routine. For example, at Führerhauptquartier Wolfsschanze where he spent a good portion of the war he would get up late and have a simple breakfast (a glass of milk and some mashed apple) with his staff in No. 1 Dining Room. This would be followed at lunchtime by a situation briefing in Keitel's bunker, which would last approximately 90 minutes. Lunch was at 1400hrs and afterwards Hitler would deal with war-related issues, but not those involving the military – war production, for example. At around 1700hrs Hitler would break for tea and cake before the next briefing chaired by Jodl at 1800hrs. This was followed by dinner at 1930hrs. Afterwards Hitler enjoyed talking to his immediate staff about non-war related subjects – informal gatherings that often went on into the early hours.

This relentless schedule and the accommodation that Hitler used did nothing for his health. At the start of the war Hitler had been able to oversee operations from his personal train or from light and airy log cabins in the heart of the countryside. Indeed for much of the early fighting in France the weather was so benign and the threat from the enemy so insignificant that he was able to be outside for much of the time. However, on the Eastern Front he had to spend increasingly lengthy periods of time in concrete bunkers so as to reduce the threat from bombing and paratrooper attack, about which he became increasingly paranoid. He was also driven to seek refuge in his bunker by the heat and the mosquitoes. Hitler later complained that they had found for him, 'The swampiest, most climatically unfavourable and midge-infested region possible'. But this troglodytic life did not suit Hitler. Even as early as August 1941 Christa Schroeder noted that 'The boss does not look at all well, he gets too little fresh air and is now oversensitive to sun and wind whenever he goes for a few hours' drive'.

In the summer of 1942 he moved his headquarters to Vinnitsa in the Ukraine, but he enjoyed no respite. Below noted that 'Hitler did not feel well here. He found the heat oppressive and the place was plagued by flies and mosquitoes'. Führerhauptquartier Wehrwolf was cold at night and stiflingly warm in the day and because of the mosquitoes Hitler and his staff were forced to take vile anti-malarial drugs. These factors combined to give Hitler migraines and he was quick to lose his temper. He longed for the relative comfort of Wolfsschanze and eventually he returned to East Prussia, but he was still plagued by the summer heat. In 1944 Junge noted that 'Hitler hated this kind of [hot] weather. Blondi [his dog] was exercised almost exclusively by Sergeant Tornow the dog walker, while Hitler stayed in the cool of the concrete rooms'. In November 1944 he left Wolfsschanze for ever and after a short stay at Führerhauptquartier Adlerhorst to oversee the Ardennes Offensive he returned to Berlin. Unable to sleep or work in the Chancellery because of the constant air raids, Hitler descended into the Führerbunker – a surreal world that Speer described as the 'Isle of the Departed'. Hitler would often speak to this chief architect about the great plans they had had for the Reich. All too often these were interrupted by explosions that made the Führer jump. Speer later asked: 'What had become of the formerly fearless corporal of World War I? He was now a wreck, a bundle of nerves who could no longer conceal his reactions.'

The former schoolhouse in Brûly-de-Pesche, which today is used as a youth hostel. In 1940 the building formed part of Wolfsschlucht I and was used as offices for *Führerhauptquartier* staff. (Author)

For Hitler's inner circle, life in the *Führerhauptquartiere* was often equally depressing. The portents of what was to come were first experienced by Hitler's secretaries, Christa Schroeder and Gerda Christian when they were on the *Führersonderzug* for the campaign in Poland. While Hitler was able to take off to the front, they were obliged to stay on board and suffer the heat and boredom. Life was better at Führerhauptquartier Felsennest, set in the heart of the Eifel (albeit Schroeder still complained of the clamminess in the bunker), and was helped by the various victories which were accompanied by celebrations. These, as Warlimont was quick to point out, were unheard of at a military headquarters. Führerhauptquartier Wolfsschlucht I at Brûly-de-Pesche was also in a beautiful setting, although the accommodation was a little basic; to begin with there was no running water and Schroeder and Christian had to sleep in a pigsty that caught fire on the first night!

With France defeated, Hitler's staff enjoyed a short respite from the claustrophobic atmosphere of headquarters life. But once the plans for the invasion of the Soviet Union had been finalized Hitler and his staff moved to FHQ Wolfsschanze in East Prussia. Initially the new headquarters was well received – the weather was fine and the surroundings beautiful, but as their stay lengthened perceptions changed. The daily routine became monotonous, and with so little to do (for the secretaries at least) time dragged. To make matters worse the *Führerhauptquartier* staff rarely changed and familiarity began to breed contempt as weeks turned into months. Christa Schroeder summed up her experience thus: 'I often feel so feckless and superfluous here. If I consider what I actually do all day the shattering answer is: absolutely nothing... We eat, we drink, we sleep, now and then we type a bit, and meantime keep him [Hitler] company for hours on end.'

Her mood was not helped by the accommodation, which was rudimentary. She was forced to sleep in a cold and damp bunker with no windows and where fresh air was provided through a ventilation system. However, 'Because the noise from the fan in the bunker disturbed us ... we requested that it be turned off at night with the consequence that we now sleep in a fug and suffer all next day from leaden heaviness in the limbs.' In

Whilst the wooden blockhouses and concrete bunkers at FHQ Wehrwolf were demolished or destroyed, the swimming pool survived and today is home to various aquatic plants. (E. Hitriak and I. Volkov)

the end Schroeder started to sleep in the office, which at least had a window. But, if nothing else, the bunkers were cool and provided respite from the summer heat, and also afforded some sanctuary from the swarms of insects that were prevalent; Schroeder was badly bitten on her legs, which swelled up. The military were slightly better protected with their boots, their uniforms and hats, but even then they would often wear mosquito nets. A member of Jodl's staff noted in a letter: 'We are being plagued by the most awful mosquitoes. It would be hard to pick a more senseless site than this – deciduous forest with marshy pools, sandy ground and stagnant lakes, ideal for these loathsome creatures.'

Life at FHQ Wehrwolf was a little better. The food was plentiful and good and security was not an issue (in the early days at least). As Warlimont noted, 'The civil population [around Vinnitsa] was still there both in town and countryside and in general appeared friendly. We used to walk unescorted through the woods and swim in the River Bug and there were never any incidents'. Small bunkers were provided for air raids, but Hitler and his staff were accommodated in wooden cabins or huts. On arriving at FHQ Wehrwolf the secretaries were full of optimism having survived so long in the dank, dark bunkers of the 'Wolf's Lair', but their hopes were dashed by what they found. Schroeder noted in a letter that 'Her depression got worse [Johanna Wolf], and mine began, when we saw our office'.

Things though did improve gradually. Below noted on his return to FHQ Wolfsschanze in November 1942 that wooden annexes had been fitted to the bunkers which made them more habitable, and Hitler had a new study for conferences. Also a cinema was built and a *Teehaus* which made life bearable. But this improvement was short lived. In February 1944 work began to strengthen the buildings against air attack. This was not complete when Hitler and his entourage were forced to return to FHQ Wolfsschanze in the summer of that year and the peace that was so jealously guarded was

Life in the *Führerhauptquartier* carried on much as normal. Here, some of Hitler's courtiers celebrate the birthday of Oberstleutnant Below, Hitler's Luftwaffe adjutant, at FHQ Wehrwolf in September 1942. The guest of honour can be seen with his back to the camera next to Johanna Wolf. (Topfoto)

lost. Security was also compromised and indeed one of the construction workers was suspected of planting the 20 July bomb that injured Hitler and as a result the already stringent security was tightened further. As early as August 1941 Christa Schroeder was complaining that she would 'come up eternally against sentries, eternally have to show our identity papers, which makes one feel trapped'. After the 20 July assassination attempt and with the Red Army fast approaching, Traudl Junge complained that 'There were barriers and new guard posts everywhere, mines, tangles of barbed wire, watchtowers. The paths along which I had walked my dog one day would suddenly be blocked the next with a guard wanting to see my pass'.

In spite of everything, the return to FHQ Wolfsschanze in the summer of 1944 was welcomed by some staff members. In July 1944 Karl Thöt, a stenographer, noted in his diary that, 'The whole site is resplendent with luscious greenery. The woods breathe a magnificent tranquillity'. And in spite of all the privations, some of Hitler's staff enjoyed their time at FHQ Wolfsschanze. In the autumn of 1944 Junge left in a melancholy mood noting, 'I had enjoyed my life in the forest, and had taken the landscape of East Prussia to my heart'. And Junge's mood was not dampened by her next accommodation at FHQ Adlerhorst which she arrived at in late December 1944. She recounted that, 'It was a beautiful place. Little log cabins clung to the wooded slopes… The rooms were smaller, but better furnished.'

This idyllic interlude was short-lived, however, and in January 1945 Hitler and his staff returned to the relative safety of Berlin. Initially they stayed in the shattered grandeur of the Reich Chancellery but were soon forced to seek refuge in the subterranean bunkers. These were never designed for anything more than a short stay but now the *Vorbunker* and *Führerbunker* were pressed into use as an improvised headquarters. Light was supplied by naked light bulbs powered by a generator, which sometimes cut out, plunging everything into darkness. Fire hoses were laid along the corridors and served as improvised water mains. The ventilation system was overstretched, used as it was to provide fresh air for the bunker and the emergency dressing station under the Chancellery. With the thick smoke and dust outside it was sometimes turned off to avoid pumping noxious fumes into the bunker. The intermittent ventilation system, combined with fumes from the generator, cigarette smoke, fumes from alcohol and perspiration created an unsavoury mix for the residents of the bunker.

But the fetid air was a minor irritant when compared with the danger presented by enemy bombing. Junge noted: 'In the evening, punctual as clockwork, enemy aircraft came over, and we had to dine with Hitler in the little room in the bunker where he lived and worked.' This bombing and shelling caused bits of concrete to crumble from the walls and the roof of the *Vorbunker* was holed in a number of places, allowing water in. But in spite of all this some occupants were still able to joke: 'Someone said Berlin was a very practical spot for headquarters, because soon we'd be able to travel between the Eastern Front and the Western Front by suburban railway.'

Ironically it was in Berlin that the various *Führerhauptquartiere* used by Hitler were designed. The task was assigned to Siegfried Schmelcher, an architect, who worked for the OT. He and his small team were responsible for all facets of the construction from sewerage to camouflage. At the outset the works programme was relatively small and construction work could be managed by German OT workers and domestic contractors. However, as the scale of the work and the geographic spread of the projects grew, foreign

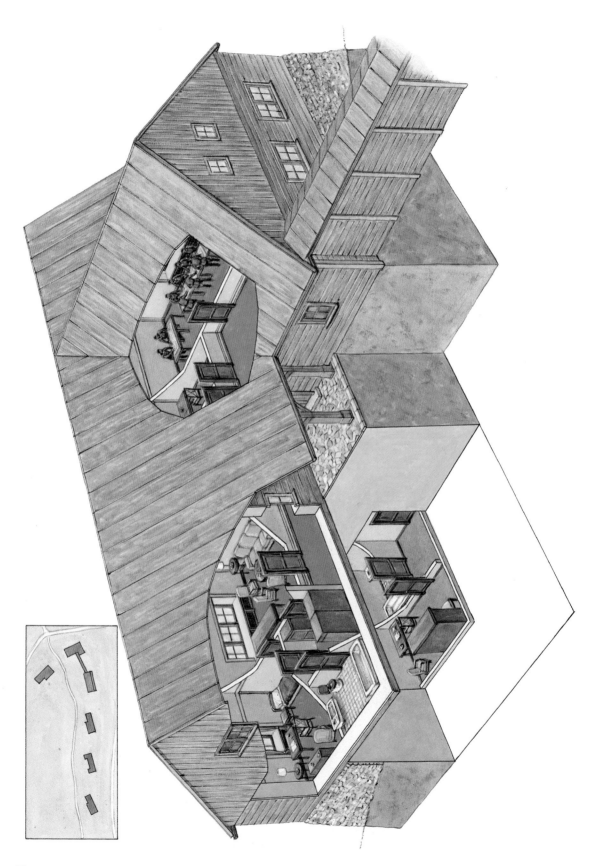

A view of the largest bunker at Wolfsschlucht II, which was later renamed 'Constance'. The long shot demonstrates how enormous the structure was. (Author)

Most of Hitler's headquarters were constructed by German workers of the OT. However, FHQ Wehrwolf, which was located deep inside the Soviet Union, was built with forced labour, including prisoners of war. Many of these died in the process and a memorial was erected to their memory after the war. (Topfoto)

F ADLERHORST, BAD NAUHEIM

On 11 December 1944 Hitler arrived at FHQ Adlerhorst, but rather than the splendour of the Schloß Ziegenberg, which had been renovated for his use, Hitler occupied one of the six specially constructed fortified houses a kilometre to the rear near the village of Wiesental. Hitler's house consisted of a large bunker, the upper edge of which protruded just above the ground and was faced with natural stone. On top of the bunker was a Swiss-style chalet clad in timber.

Built in an 'L' shape, Hitler's bedroom, bathroom and dressing room were located at the far end. Next door was Hitler's study,

which could be accessed from his private quarters or from the corridor. The corridor continued to a large ante-room from where it was possible to gain access to the outside and the cellar as well the map room, the recreation room, two of the adjutant's rooms (the other two could be accessed from the corridor) and the toilets.

The cellar was almost an exact copy of the upper floor. Stairs led down to the gas lock and then a corridor. At the far end were Hitler's private rooms and next to these were a further map room and office and a room for the ventilation system.

labourers had to be conscripted. So, in the Soviet Union, local labourers were used to construct FHQ Wehrwolf and similarly, on FHQ Wolfsschlucht II French workers were employed. In Silesia the sheer scale of work involved in the building of FHQ Riese necessitated the use of not just OT workers, but also 50,000–60,000 concentration-camp inmates from the nearby Gross Rosen camp.

The use of foreign labourers posed an additional threat to Hitler's security, which was the responsibility of various police and military units. The job of guarding Hitler when he travelled by train or motorcade was the responsibility of the Führer Begleit Bataillon (FBB). Most of the men of this unit were recruited from Infanterie-Regiment Grossdeutschland and until January 1940 the unit was under the command of one Erwin Rommel, later to earn fame as the Desert Fox.

With the decision to use a permanent headquarters for future operations, the role of the FBB was expanded to include the job of reconnoitring suitable sites. Moreover, once the *Führerhauptquartier* was complete the FBB was responsible for protecting the site against commando-style attacks or airborne assaults and, more mundanely, against general intruders. To do this the men of the FBB patrolled the perimeter fence (sometimes in plain clothes) and manned the watchtowers. Motorised troops patrolled further afield. Unsurprisingly for a unit assigned to guard the Führer it was extremely well equipped with all the most modern weapons.

While their primary concern was the security of the Führer, elements of the FBB were sent to the eastern front for combat training and indeed in the first rotation in the autumn of 1941 the unit was involved in heavy fighting before the men returned to FHQ Wolfsschanze. This rotation continued throughout the war and meant that the unit was effectively almost two battalions in strength.

In September 1944, following the failed July plot, the FBB was expanded and became known as the Führer Begleit Regiment. This was a further shift towards the unit becoming a fully fledged fighting unit rather than simply a security organisation, its ability to undertake this role having been brought into question by the devastating bomb blast. In November 1944 it was enlarged still further and became the Führer Begleit Brigade. By now the unit was a fully functioning fighting unit and in January 1945 it was made into a division and fought in the Ardennes before being withdrawn to fight on the eastern front where it was encircled and destroyed.

While the FBB was responsible for external security the Reichssicherheitsdienst (RSD – Reich Security Service) was responsible for internal security. It was split into a series of agencies with Dienststelle 1 (Bureau 1) specifically responsible for the Führer's security. At the outbreak of war RSD strength stood at around 200 men, but during the course of the conflict the numbers swelled so that by the end of the war it had doubled in number. The vast majority were recruited from Bavaria and often from the police force there. Being principally made up of former police officers the focus of their work was investigative – gathering intelligence on possible threats – and preventative – checking routes and venues that Hitler would use. Reichssicherheitsdienst officers were also responsible for vetting workers involved in the construction of Hitler's headquarters and when complete they were responsible for security inside the various *Führerhauptquartiere*.

They were given SS ranks and wore SS uniform, unless they were under cover, when they wore civilian clothes. They were commanded by SS

Gruppenführer Johann Rattenhuber, with Hitler, not Himmler, in overall command and he personally approved all appointments.

The SS Begleit Kommando (SS Escort Detachment) – not to be confused with the Führer Begleit Bataillon – provided the Führer's personal security. The unit had its origins in the earliest history of the Nazi Party. In 1933 the SS Leibstandarte (SS Bodyguard Regiment) was formed under the command of Sepp Dietrich and uniquely, although an SS unit, it reported to Hitler not Himmler. From this regiment were drawn the men for the elite SS Begleit Kommando.

The genesis of the SS Begleit Kommando can actually be traced back to 1932 when eight SS members were selected to act as Hitler's personal bodyguards. By the time Hitler invaded Russia in June 1941 it had risen to 35 and by the beginning of 1943 it had swelled to 143 officers and men. Only 33 were involved in the personal security of the Führer, the rest looked after his affairs at his other residences.

As well as Hitler's personal security, the SS Begleit Kommando was responsible for protecting Hitler's bunker (with RSD personnel patrolling the exterior). But they were also responsible for many of the Führer's day to day needs including looking after his personal possessions, preparing his clothes, taking him messages and newspapers and receiving flowers and gifts from well wishers.

Note: to confuse matters still further, when Hitler was on trips equal numbers of RSD and SS Begleit Kommando staff accompanied him and this combined unit was known as the Führer Begleit Kommando, though both units fiercely maintained their independence.

Hitler oversaw the invasion of Poland not from a permanent *Führerhauptquartier*, but from his personal train 'Amerika'. Here the Führer is flanked by adjutants Schmundt (right) and Engel (left). In the left foreground Generalfeldmarschall Brauchitsch and Generalfeldmarschall Keitel are in discussion. (Topfoto)

OPERATIONAL HISTORY

Operation *Weiss*

On 1 September 1939 the German training ship *Schleswig-Holstein*, anchored in Danzig harbour, opened fire on the Polish garrison stationed in the historic city and in so doing signalled the start of World War II in Europe. Concurrently Luftwaffe aircraft attacked Polish airbases and other strategic targets and German land forces crossed the border in accordance with the plans of Operation *Weiss* (White). Some 60 divisions attacked the much smaller Polish Army from Pomerania and East Prussia in the north and Silesia in the south, using the previously untested blitzkrieg technique.

The campaign was planned and directed by the German Army, but was the realization of Hitler's strategy and he planned to keep a close eye on developments from his personal train – Führersonderzug 'Amerika'. On 3 September, with the declarations of war from Britain and France ringing in his ears, Hitler set off for Bad Polzin in Pomerania, arriving in the early hours of 4 September. For the next fortnight of the campaign the *Führersonderzug* shuttled along the eastern border of Germany, and Hitler, either in a convoy of vehicles or in a light aircraft, toured the front, seeing at first hand the awesome power of the Wehrmacht as it crushed the brave resistance of the inferior Polish forces.

On 17 September Hitler returned to Berlin to ensure that he was well out of the way when the Soviets crossed into eastern Poland in accordance with the German–Soviet Treaty of Non-Aggression. But Hitler was not to be cowed for long and on 18 September he rejoined the *Führersonderzug*, this time as it headed for the historic city of Danzig, where the war had started and where the mainly German population was sure to give him a warm welcome – and so it did. Having set up his new headquarters at the Casino Hotel in Zoppot, he set off in a motorcade for Danzig, where he was greeted as a liberator.

The Casino Hotel served as Hitler's headquarters until 25 September when he returned to Berlin, and it was here that he received the news of the fall of Warsaw on 27 September and the end of organized resistance on 5 October. Yet in spite of the fact that the Poles had been crushed in a little over a month it was clear that there were a number of serious shortcomings in the way the operation had been executed. One of the most significant was that trains (and hotels) were not suitable to act as the Führer's headquarters. This deficiency had been recognized as early as 10 September when Rommel was dispatched to identify the location of a permanent headquarters in the west. Eventually Hitler chose FHQ Felsennest, in the heart of the Eifel, because it was located near the Ardennes – the *Schwerpunkt* (main emphasis) of the attack.

Operation *Gelb*

On the night of 9 May 1940, the eve of the offensive in the west, Hitler boarded his train

Hitler leaves his camouflaged bunker at FHQ Felsennest. He is followed by his adjutant Nicolas von Below. Just visible on the left is a camouflaged door that would have been closed to avoid detection by enemy planes. White hoops around the base of the trees helped people navigate around the site in the dark. (Topfoto)

and set off from Berlin towards FHQ Felsennest. However, to avoid suspicion the train first headed north before swinging west and arriving at Euskirchen where Hitler alighted and headed for the village of Rodert, protected by a detachment of the FBB. He arrived at his *Führerhauptquartier* in the early hours of the morning and Christa Schroeder, one of his secretaries, recounted that 'As we stood near the bunker at dawn we could hear artillery fire in the distance. Hitler gestured with his hand towards the west and said: "Meine Herren, the offensive against the western powers has just begun"'. At almost the same time German paratroopers in gliders were landing at Fort Eben Emael – the keystone to the Belgian defences. Using hollow charges, engineers of Sturmabteilung Koch destroyed a number of emplacements and kept the garrison sufficiently occupied that airborne troops were able to capture key bridges across the Albert canal. Fittingly, Hauptmann Koch and his officers received their decorations from Hitler on 16 May at FHQ Felsennest.

The German attack prompted a rapid response from the French and British, who pressed north to meet the threat safe in the knowledge that their flank was protected by the impregnable Maginot Line and the impassable forest of the Ardennes. However, their faith was misplaced and German armour carefully edged along the narrow forest roads and massed on the east bank of the River Meuse. On 13 May lead elements crossed the river and thereafter the Panzers quickly advanced towards the Channel, reaching Abbeville on the coast on 20 May and in so doing cutting the line of retreat for the bulk of the British and French forces.

Indeed, so expeditious was the advance that Hitler asked that a suitable location be identified farther west so that he was better able to direct operations. An abandoned Maginot Line bunker near Maubeuge was identified as a possible location, but was considered too small. Instead a small village in Belgium – Brûly-de-Pesche – was chosen. With the local population resettled, the OT moved in and on 6 June 1940 Hitler arrived at the newly christened 'Wolfsschlucht'.

By this time Belgium had surrendered (on 28 May) and the British Expeditionary Force (BEF) had evacuated the bulk of its men in what became known as the 'miracle of Dunkirk'. The French Army continued to fight, falling back to the so-called 'Weygand Line' where they stubbornly resisted against German attacks. However, once this line was pierced there was nothing to stop the German advance and Paris was captured on 14 June, whilst the forts of the Maginot Line were systematically reduced from the rear. Three days later the Germans were approached by the French seeking peace terms. Hitler was at Wolfsschlucht I when he heard the news from Walter Hewel, Ribbentrop's representative at the *Führerhauptquartier*, and the Führer could not disguise his delight – a scene that was captured on film.

The wrongs of the Paris Peace Settlement had been rectified. On 22 June France was forced to sign a humiliating armistice in the same railway carriage at Compiègne that had been used to take the German surrender in November 1918. To complete the humiliation Hitler took a whirlwind tour of Paris on 23 June but was back at Wolfsschlucht by mid-morning.

From here Hitler now moved to FHQ Tannenberg, one of the four headquarters that had been readied for the campaign in the west. From here he visited some of the battlefields of World War I where he served as a *Gefreiter* and inspected some of the Maginot Line fortifications as well as visiting injured troops in hospital.

Hitler's personal train, 'Amerika', was used as his headquarters once again for the invasion of the Balkans in April 1941. Here Hitler can be seen discussing plans with Generalfeldmarschall Brauchitsch and Generalfeldmarschall Keitel. (Topfoto)

Hitler's next destination should have been FHQ Adlerhorst, where plans for the invasion of Britain were being prepared. However, a brave rearguard action and Hitler's decision to halt Rundstedt's Panzers on 24 May meant that the bulk of the BEF was successfully evacuated across the beaches of Dunkirk, and although lacking heavy weapons they represented a considerable threat to an amphibious attack. More significantly, Göring's Luftwaffe had signally failed to cow the RAF, which meant that any landing would not have air superiority – a factor that was vital for success. As a result Operation *Seelöwe* (Sea Lion) was postponed and eventually cancelled. Finally, on 5 July Hitler boarded the *Führersonderzug* and steamed to Berlin, where he received a hero's welcome. But what he did not realize was that the next time he visited his western headquarters it would be to direct operations to meet an Allied invasion, not launch his own.

The Balkan campaign

With plans for the invasion of Britain cancelled, Hitler now concentrated all his energy on plans for the invasion of the Soviet Union and securing *Lebensraum* for the German people. However, his plans were interrupted by the difficulties of his main ally in the Balkans. On 28 October 1940 Italy had invaded Greece from bases in Albania, but the attack was repulsed and the Greek Army went on the offensive. Concerned by this reverse, but also keen to protect the Romanian oilfields and his southern flank in any attack on the Soviet Union, Hitler ordered plans to be prepared for an invasion of the Balkans. At the beginning of March 1941 the Italians renewed their attack but without success, and a month later the Germans launched Operation *Frühlingssturm* (Spring Storm) – the invasion of Yugoslavia and Greece. With no time to prepare a permanent headquarters, Hitler once again used Führersonderzug 'Amerika', with the WFSt on Sonderzug 'Atlas'. On 11 April 1941, five days after the start of the operation, 'Atlas' pulled into Mönichkirchen on the main line between Vienna and Graz. The village was chosen because of its location and because it was near a rail tunnel that could be used to shelter the train in the event of air attack. The station itself was small and was adapted with the erection of makeshift platforms and the establishment of a signals station. On the following day Hitler's train arrived and, aside from a few walks to a nearby hotel, this is where Hitler stayed for the whole of the short campaign – even celebrating his 52nd birthday there. On 26 April, with the Yugoslav and Greek forces defeated and the British and Commonwealth troops evacuating the Greek peninsula, Hitler entrained for Berlin where plans for the next, and most demanding, campaign were well advanced.

Operation *Barbarossa*

After a number of delays, Operation *Barbarossa* – the German invasion of the Soviet Union – was launched on 22 June 1941. The plan was simple; three army groups would advance on Leningrad, Moscow and the Ukraine respectively with the aim of destroying the Red Army. Generalfeldmarschall Brauchitsch was in overall command, but Hitler took a close personal interest and on 24 June arrived at FHQ Wolfsschanze in East Prussia.

Hitler's forces, using the blitzkrieg technique that had been so devastating in Poland and the west, smashed through the new western defences constructed by the Soviets following the defeat of Poland and headed deep into Russia. By the middle of July, Smolensk – the gateway to Moscow – had been captured and little seemingly stood between Hitler's forces and the Soviet capital. Now, however, Hitler changed his strategy. Army Group Centre went on the defensive and priority was given to the drives north and south. By the end of August the northern thrust had broken through the old Stalin Line defences and was closing on Leningrad, the birthplace of the revolution, while in the south Rundstedt's Army Group had reached the River Dnieper and Kiev, the capital of Ukraine.

Hitler now took time out to visit another of his headquarters on the eastern front – Anlage Süd – and held talks with Mussolini who had travelled

Unusually for most of the *Führerhauptquartiere*, the site at Vinnitsa, where FHQ Wehrwolf was located, is easily accessible with good views of all of the remains. (E. Hitriak and I. Volkov)

In June 1944 Hitler travelled to Wolfsschlucht II to discuss the Allied landings with his generals. They were protected from Allied air attack by the massive concrete roof of the *Führerbunker*. In the foreground is a red brick chimney. (Author)

east on his personal train. Their discussions complete, Hitler returned to FHQ Wolfsschanze where, at the end of September, he received news of the encirclement of Kiev. Convinced now that the Red Army was beaten Hitler decided to make a final bid to capture Moscow in 1941. However, the hiatus had enabled the Muscovites to strengthen their defences around the capital and determined resistance brought the advance to a standstill. Subsequent attempts were made to renew the attack but bad weather and exhaustion meant that the advance had to halt just 30km from the city. With the enemy overextended, the Red Army launched a surprise counter-attack that pushed the Germans back and ensured the safety of the capital. The failure to capture this key objective so incensed Hitler that on 19 December he relieved Brauchitsch of his role as Oberbefehlshaber des Heeres (Commander-in-Chief of the Army) and he assumed the role himself.

Operation *Blau*

By the winter of 1941 Hitler's forces had reached Moscow, had all but encircled Leningrad and in the south had captured the Donets Basin. And it was in the south that Hitler's focus centred on the summer offensive planned for 1942. Because the offensive was so far removed from FHQ Wolfsschanze, a new site was identified near Vinnitsa in the Ukraine. From here Hitler could

G BERLIN BUNKER

With the failure of the Ardennes Offensive, Hitler left FHQ Adlerhorst on 15 January 1945 and returned to Berlin. The city was much changed, having sustained months of heavy Allied bombing. The Reich Chancellery buildings were no longer safe, so Hitler and his staff retreated to the bunkers beneath. These had not been designed for permanent occupation but rather as a short-term refuge from isolated air raids.

In spite of the danger, Hitler insisted that he would stay in the capital rather than flee to the relative safety of southern Germany. Unable to change his mind, his staff now took steps to make this last bastion more habitable. Improvised telecommunication, ventilation, water and power systems were installed to enable the Führer to govern the shrinking Reich. But conditions in the bunker were still grim and grew steadily worse as the Red Army

firstly encircled the city and then slowly advanced on the Reich Chancellery. Some of Hitler's most trusted followers now took their leave and fled to other parts of Germany, but others stayed on, determined to be with the Führer to the bitter end.

On 30 April 1945 Hitler and Eva Braun committed suicide in the bunker, and their bodies were burned in the garden outside. Goebbels and his wife took the same route out after having callously killed their children. With their leader dead the remaining staff escaped from the bunker and tried to break through the Soviet lines with differing levels of success. Some perished, others were captured by the Soviets and spent many years in captivity and still others reached the relative safety of the western Allies, where they were tried and punished according to their crimes.

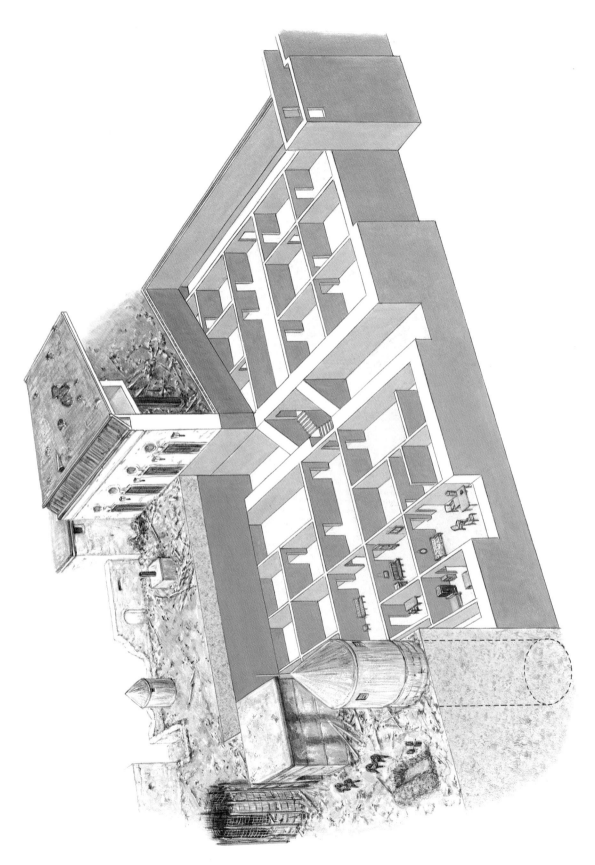

The largest bunker at Wolfsschlucht II was some 90m in length. It was captured by the Allies and after the war it was used by the Americans. The building was christened 'Constance' but when the author visited in 2009 the name appeared to have changed to 'Patricia'. (Author)

better direct operations towards Stalingrad and the Caucasus. In April 1942 Hitler issued the directive for Operation *Blau* (Blue), and on 28 June the first phase of the operation was launched. Soon thereafter (16 July) Hitler and his staff moved to FHQ Wehrwolf. Progress was good with Army Group A advancing into the Caucasus and elements of Army Group B entering the city of Stalingrad in mid-September. Confident that his forces in the south would soon capture the city that bore the name of his ideological enemy, he departed Wehrwolf on 1 November for Wolfsschanze. In East Prussia he would be better able to direct operations personally against any Soviet winter offensive, which he confidently predicted would be launched on the northern or central fronts. His conviction could not have been farther from the truth. On 19 November the Red Army launched a counter-offensive (Operation *Uranus*) that encircled the German troops fighting in Stalingrad. Hitler refused Paulus' request to break out and instead set about mustering a force to relieve the troops trapped in the pocket. The relief operation was launched but was unsuccessful and on 31 January 1943 Paulus (now a *Generalfeldmarschall*) surrendered, much to Hitler's chagrin.

With the German southern advance decisively stopped and the Red Army on the attack, Hitler reinstated Army Group South and on 17 February 1943 returned to FHQ Wehrwolf to witness Manstein's spring offensive. At the end of February, 4. Armee, under Hoth, advanced north from its position on the River Dnieper and, in spite of the thaw, recaptured Kharkov on 11 March.

Operation *Citadel*

Hitler now began preparations for the German summer offensive and such was the air of optimism that permeated FHQ Wolfsschanze that plans were drawn up for a new headquarters – FHQ Olga – near Vitebsk. However, this optimism proved misplaced. On 5 July Operation *Citadel* was launched and initially the two arms of the great pincer around the Kursk salient made good progress, but having had time to prepare deep defences and with good intelligence spelling out German intentions, the offensive stalled. This coincided with worrying developments in Italy, where the Allies had landed in Sicily on 10 July, and on 13 July Hitler cancelled Operation *Citadel*.

At the end of August the Soviets launched a series of offensives that pinched out the Orel and Kharkov salients. From this point forward the Red Army held the initiative, and Hitler and his generals ensconced in the bunkers of FHQ Wolfsschanze knew this.

On 27 August Hitler visited Manstein at FHQ Wehrwolf. Here he received a gloomy situation report; without reinforcements the Donets Basin would have to be conceded. Hitler promised to provide whatever units were available, before returning to Rastenburg that evening. This was to be Hitler's last visit to his headquarters in the Ukraine.

With no reinforcements available, Hitler reluctantly agreed that Army Group South should withdraw to the River Dnieper, but crossing points were limited and this meant that the broad front fractured. The Soviets took advantage of this, racing to cross the river using any means available and soon a number of bridgeheads had been created, which by December had developed into two significant bulges around Kiev and to the south around Cherkassy, Kremenchung and Dnepropetrovsk. On 28 December 1943 Hitler ordered that FHQ Wehrwolf be demolished.

In the north the blockade of Leningrad was lifted at the end of January 1944 and Army Group North was forced back to the so-called Panther Line which ran along the River Narva, Lake Peipus and Lake Pskov. The Soviet offensive in the centre was hampered by adverse weather conditions and a general lack of preparation, and little progress was made save for the encirclement of six German divisions – many of which ultimately extricated themselves.

This concluded the winter offensive and at the end of February 1944 Hitler departed Wolfsschanze for Berchtesgaden. The Soviets continued to apply pressure throughout the spring while at the same time planning for a major summer offensive. Hitler meantime had already stressed to his generals that the Eastern Front was a secondary concern. Territory could be conceded in the east but not in the west, where the Allied invasion was considered imminent. More immediately troops had to be sent from the Russian front to Italy to counter the Allied invasion of Sicily and Italy (which began on 3 September 1943). In April 1944 Hitler celebrated another birthday – the last 'normal' celebration he would enjoy – before his 'Fortress Europe' was hit with a further hammer blow with the landings in Normandy.

D-Day

For some time Hitler had been expecting the western Allies to open a second front in France. Now, on 6 June 1944, the invasion began. Hitler received the news while at Berchtesgaden. Initially he was convinced that this was simply a diversionary attack before the main invasion around the Pas-de-Calais, but as time passed this hypothesis carried less weight and in mid-June Hitler travelled to FHQ Wolfsschlucht II at Margival in France. Here he met Rundstedt and Rommel and was briefed on the situation. Hitler insisted that they maintain their positions and reiterated this at another briefing at Berchtesgaden on 29 June. But by now he had a far greater worry with the opening of the Red Army's summer offensive.

Operation *Bagration*

On 23 June 1944 the Red Army launched Operation *Bagration*. The initial thrust was directed at Army Group Centre and was considered a feint by Hitler who instructed that the attack be held. However, in spite of the fact that Generalfeldmarschall Busch, the commander of Army Group Centre, committed all his reserves he was unable to stop the Soviet juggernaut. Hitler now realized that this was a major offensive and on 9 July he headed back to FHQ Wolfsschanze to direct operations. His eastern headquarters was still a building site, but the critical situation meant that it was vital that Hitler be close to the front to personally influence commanders in the field. But his presence could not turn the tide. Army Group Centre had all but collapsed and Generalfeldmarschall Model, who had replaced Busch, now tried to make an orderly withdrawal. In this he was broadly successful but he could not disguise the fact that Operation *Bagration* had been a major success for the Soviets. The second phase exploited these successes as the Red Army advanced towards East Prussia and crossed the River Vistula. As Warlimont noted, 'The return to the field headquarters in East Prussia meant that we were for once – just as at the same period of 1941 – unwontedly close to the front'. Now, however, Hitler's armed forces were marching west not east, and, recognizing the enormity of the situation, Germany's allies toppled like a pack of cards: on 23 August Romania surrendered, on 2 September Finland signed an armistice and on 9 September Bulgaria did likewise.

In spite of these setbacks Hitler insisted, in October, that he would remain at FHQ Wolfsschanze until the crisis had been averted. Yet only a month later, on 20 November, with the concrete hardly dry, he left Rastenburg, ostensibly to oversee the imminent offensive in the west, but equally to avoid being cut off by the advancing Red Army.

Ardennes Offensive

Although the situation at the end of 1944 was perilous, Hitler still managed to muster sufficient reserves to launch one last offensive in the west, which he hoped would deliver a decisive victory. The location he chose was the scene of his great triumph in 1940 – the Ardennes – which was weakly held by a mixture of new and recuperating US divisions.

On 10 December Hitler arrived at FHQ Adlerhorst to direct the attack personally. The following day he briefed his commanders, explaining in a long speech the military and political imperatives for the attack. Finally, on 16 December 6. SS-Panzer-Armee, 5. Panzer-Armee and 7. Armee advanced. Their target was the port of Antwerp, which if captured would split the Allies'

H ASSASSINATION ATTEMPT, 20 JULY 1944

In the period after Hitler came to power several attempts were made on his life, none of which were successful. The failure of the conspirators led Hitler to believe that he was immortal and predestined to lead Germany to victory. However, this personal conviction did nothing to discourage his enemies and a further attempt on Hitler's life was planned for the summer of 1944. The man chosen to carry out the attempt was Oberst Claus Schenk Graf von Stauffenberg. A decorated officer who had been badly injured in North Africa, he was now a staff officer with access to Hitler at FHQ Wolfsschanze.

The plan, codenamed 'Valkyrie', was simple. Stauffenberg would place a briefcase of explosives next to Hitler during one of his briefings and then make his excuses to leave. The bomb would explode, killing Hitler and his immediate circle of advisers. With the Führer dead the conspirators would cut communications to FHQ Wolfsschanze and seize key locations throughout the Reich.

The bomb exploded as planned, but unbeknown to Stauffenberg, who had left the room and was now heading to Berlin, Hitler survived, receiving only minor injuries. The failure of the bomb to eliminate its prime target was partly due to the fact that Stauffenberg had not had time to pack all the explosives in the case and partly because the briefing was held in a timber-lined barrack block rather than Hitler's reinforced concrete bunker, which was still being renovated. The explosion was thus much smaller than planned and the blast was dissipated through the hut's walls and windows.

Hitler was badly shaken by the explosion and three of his staff were killed, but he was alive and with communication links still open he was able to confirm that he was safe and well and his supporters were able to quickly round up the conspirators, who were executed, often in a most gruesome fashion and filmed for the Führer's delectation.

front in half. Initially progress was good with the enemy caught completely by surprise and cloud cover preventing the Allies interdicting the German ground forces.

Though initially caught off balance, the Allies soon recovered and rapidly instigated plans to counter the attack. In this they were undoubtedly helped by the fact that Hitler decided to exploit the advance of 5. Panzer-Armee too late, and by the time action was taken clearing skies exposed the German units to air attack, which further hampered the already fragile logistics operation.

By Christmas Day the German bulge extended 95km at its deepest, but with supplies exhausted they could go no farther and on 3 January the Allies launched a counter-attack to pinch out the bulge. Hodges' First US Army, which had borne the brunt of the attack, drove into the northern flank while Patton's Third US Army advanced to meet it at Houffalize. Heavy snow slowed the advance and the pocket was not closed until 16 January, by which time most of the German troops had escaped. But the damage done to the German Army and Luftwaffe was irreparable. His gamble having failed Hitler left FHQ Adlerhorst for Berlin on 15 January and prepared for the final *Götterdämmerung*.

Berlin

Although Hitler's adversaries saw Berlin as the ultimate symbol of Nazism, Hitler in fact spent relatively little time in the capital, preferring instead his field headquarters, principally FHQ Wolfsschanze or his Alpine retreat at Berchtesgaden. However, by the end of the war his choice of locations was severely limited and after the failure of the Ardennes offensive the Führer returned to Berlin. It was in the Reich Chancellery that he decided to see out the last days of the war, in spite of the protestations of some of his closest aides who wanted him to flee abroad or to Bavaria.

A picture taken after the war inside the Führerbunker in Berlin. The US soldier inspects Hitler's bed and to the right is his safe. This was badly damaged when the Soviets tried to cut it open. (Topfoto)

Already by 15 April Soviet forces under Konev, Rokossovsky and Zhukov had reached the River Oder, which at its nearest point was only 55km from the capital. Zhukov, who had been given the honour of capturing Berlin by Stalin, now set about launching a *coup de main* across the Seelow Heights, but in spite of a massive superiority in men and *matériel* his advance was held. At the behest of Stalin he now changed the point of the attack and swung north while Konev advanced from the south. The pincers closed around the beleaguered city on 25 April and the battle of Berlin began in earnest.

Hitler now retired to the relative safety of the bunker under the Chancellery, but even this was not immune. Loringhoven recalled that: 'In the concrete block of the Führerbunker we felt the vibrations of the uninterrupted thunder of Russian artillery as it pounded the Chancellery. The ceiling of the Vorbunker, much less thick, was in danger of collapsing under the shelling.' German units within the city, supplemented by old men and boys of the Volkssturm (People's Army), bravely resisted the onslaught, but resistance was futile. Hitler was informed that the situation was hopeless and on 30 April Hitler and his new wife Eva Braun committed suicide in the bunker. Their bodies were carried out of the subterranean gloom into the small garden

On 20 July 1944 Claus Schenk von Stauffenberg, a disillusioned young officer, planted a bomb at Hitler's East Prussian headquarters that was intended to kill the Führer. The bomb detonated, killing three, but Hitler survived, his life saved in part by the fact that the briefing was held in a temporary conference room, which absorbed some of the blast. (Topfoto)

at the rear, where they were incinerated. Other bunker inhabitants variously committed suicide or made a break for freedom. Somewhat amusingly the bunker was captured by a group of Soviet female soldiers interested only in the wardrobe of the Führer's wife. Only later did intelligence officers reach the final resting place of the Führer to begin the long investigation into his death. On 2 May Generalleutnant Weidling surrendered the city and on 7–8 May Germany unconditionally surrendered.

After the unsuccessful assassination attempt on 20 July 1944, Hitler made a radio broadcast to the nation to reassure the people that he was fit and well. His audience at FHQ Wolfsschanze consisted of his closest advisers, including personal adjutant Julius Schaub in front of the curtains. (Topfoto)

AFTERMATH

The fate of the various *Führerhauptquartiere* waxed and waned in parallel with the fortunes of the Third Reich. Führerhauptquartier Felsennest, for example, was given to the Nazi Party after the fall of France so that, as Hitler directed, it could be transformed into a national monument as a permanent reminder to future generations of the great victory. Ultimately, Hitler's wish was never fulfilled and as Patton's Third Army threatened to overrun the position it was destroyed. This was typical of the *Führerhauptquartiere* in Germany. After the defeat of France, Hitler visited FHQ Tannenberg. Afterwards, it was handed over to V Armeekorps and later, in 1944, it was once again considered as a potential *Führerhauptquartier*, but the idea was dismissed and with the Allies approaching it was demolished.

Having been dismissed by Hitler as a possible headquarters for the invasion of France, FHQ Adlerhorst was completed and identified as a possible headquarters for the invasion of Britain. However, when the operation was postponed and then cancelled the facility was mothballed and was not used again until the winter of 1944 when Hitler used it to oversee the Ardennes offensive. At the end of the war the site was destroyed by the Americans and the area redeveloped. Similarly, FHQ Waldwiese was captured by elements of 76th Infantry division and in the summer of 1946 engineers demolished the three bunkers.

The fate of the Führerbunker in Berlin is well documented. With Hitler dead, the remaining staff prepared to leave the bunker. SS Brigadeführer Mohnke, in charge of the inner defensive sector of Berlin and one of Hitler's most loyal followers, ordered that the Führerbunker be incinerated. Petrol was poured in Hitler's study and set ablaze, but with the ventilation system off and the airtight door closed the fire soon went out and did little more than char some of the furniture. With all of Hitler's staff gone only Hentschel, responsible for maintaining the bunker, remained. He was later taken prisoner by the Soviets and the empty bunker thereafter became both a ghoulish tourist attraction – with the victorious Allies (including Churchill) visiting the place

A close-up of the I-beams that formed part of the roof of the bunker under the Reich Chancellery in Berlin. Still clearly visible on one of the beams is the name Krupp – the German steel producer that manufactured the steel girders. (W. Fleischer)

After the war the Soviets tried to demolish the Führerbunker in Berlin, but with limited success. Here the observation/ventilation tower with conical roof and blockhouse above the exit lie on their sides. The photograph was taken in 1956. (Topfoto)

where Hitler died – and a crime scene as Stalin tried to establish what happened to his ideological enemy in the last days of April 1945. This included using the bunker for a full reconstruction of Hitler's last days. Finally, in 1947 the Soviets tried to demolish the bunker with some success, but it was not until 1988 that it was completely sealed up and the site redeveloped.

In occupied Europe the fortunes of the *Führerhauptquartiere* were similarly mixed. Wolfsschlucht I was somewhat unusual in that it had formerly been a quiet Belgian village. When Hitler departed, the wooden chalets that had been specially constructed for his use were demolished and the church steeple was restored. When the inhabitants of the village returned little had changed save for a concrete air-raid shelter in the forest.

In France, Wolfsschlucht II was captured intact by the Americans in 1944 and was later adapted for their own use as a military base. When France withdrew their military from NATO the Americans left and the base remained unoccupied until 1969, when it was taken over by French commandos as a training establishment, complete with the addition of mock buildings. In 1993 the French military abandoned the site and it is now looked after by volunteers.

On the Eastern Front the fighting was uncompromising, and thus when Hitler was forced to concede territory he gave orders that it was to be of no use to the enemy – the so-called 'scorched-earth policy' – and so it was with his headquarters. When Hitler left FHQ Wehrwolf in March 1943 the facility was taken over by Army Group South and when they were forced to retreat in December 1943 Hitler was very clear in his direction: 'He [Manstein] must get out of Vinnitsa… There must be a special detachment at Vinnitsa to burn the whole headquarters down and blow it up. It is important there should be no furniture left, otherwise the Russians will send it to Moscow and put it on display. Burn the lot.'

Hitler now retreated to the relative safety of FHQ Wolfsschanze. However, by the autumn of 1944 East Prussia was threatened by the Red Army and when Hitler left for Berlin in November he did not know that he would never see it again. Hope remained that he might return and it was not until January 1945 that the *Führerhauptquartier* was demolished with explosive charges. Hans Baur, Hitler's pilot, later spoke to one of those involved in the demolition work and they conceded that it had been an extremely tough job.

LEFT
Hitler's air-raid shelter at Wolfsschlucht I, which in spite of the odd threat, was never used. This door shown led from the entrance into the body of the shelter. Directly opposite was a pistol port. It is worth comparing the modest proportions of this building with Hitler's bunker at FHQ Wolfsschanze. (Author)

RIGHT
On the opposite side of the track from Margival train station are a series of buildings that formed part of Wolfsschlucht II. Bunker 56 'Loano' was later adapted with the addition of a climbing tower for the training of commandos, which is visible at the top. (Author)

After the war the site became something of a tourist attraction for the citizens of Eastern Europe – it was extremely difficult at that time for westerners to get visas to visit. However, with little money to invest and little interest in protecting a symbol of Nazi oppression the Polish authorities allowed the site to fall into disrepair. Paradoxically, this general neglect was in many respects beneficial because it meant that the site remained undisturbed, and years after the war it was still possible to find items of interest associated with its wartime use, whereas sites in the west were often stripped bare. On the downside some of the buildings that were repairable were later adapted for use as storage facilities with little thought for the fact that this work would irreparably change the face of the site. This work was eventually stopped and gradually a thriving tourist industry grew up around the site.

In light of Hitler's scorched-earth policy it is somewhat surprising that the facilities at Anlage Süd and Anlage Mitte survived the war largely intact. Thereafter they, like so many other wartime facilities in the old Eastern Bloc, lay largely untouched and only very recently has Anlage Süd been transformed

One of the 'Type 102v' concrete bunkers protecting the rail tunnel at Stepina. The two entrances lead into the body of the shelter, which is split into two parts. This example has no loopholes and appears to have been used as a shelter. (Author)

into a museum. *Führerhauptquartier Riese* was also completely overlooked. As the end of the war neared the workers on the site were forcibly moved and local inhabitants fled in the face of the approaching Red Army. Consequently, when the Soviets captured Silesia nobody was around who could explain its purpose and the new inhabitants were more intent on building a new life than pondering the past. Only later did historians begin investigating the site in any detail.

One interesting footnote that is often overlooked is the fate of the *Führersonderzug*. This served as Hitler's headquarters in both the Polish and Balkan campaigns and was used extensively in the intervening years, and yet gets little mention in many texts on the subject. Following Hitler's return to Berlin after the failed Ardennes offensive in 1945 his train was moved to the Austrian Alps for safekeeping. General Winter and his staff used the train as a headquarters until Germany capitulated in May 1945. Thereafter, Hitler's personal carriage was destroyed, but the rest of the train survived and was moved to Pullach near Munich, where it was appropriated by the US Army. It was not until the early 1950s that it was returned to the new Deutsche Reichsbahn (German State Railway), and the carriages were still in use in the 1970s when they were finally withdrawn from service.

THE SITES TODAY

A large proportion of the *Führerhauptquartiere* were destroyed either by retreating German forces during the war, or by the Allies after the cessation of hostilities. In spite of this, and with a little research to put the place in context, there is still much to be had from a visit to these places. The sites themselves are scattered across Germany and what had been occupied Europe.

Belgium

Somewhat surprisingly considering the fact that it was twice in the 20th century the victim of German aggression, Belgium has gone to great lengths to preserve Hitler's headquarters at Brûly-de-Pesche. The village itself has been preserved much as it was when Hitler used it as a headquarters in 1940, and it is still relatively easy to compare photographs taken at the time with modern views. Almost uniquely, Hitler's bunker is still *in situ* and undamaged and two new wooden chalets – not dissimilar to the originals – have been erected and house a museum devoted to the *Führerhauptquartier* and also a wider study of the war.

Opening times and entry charges can be found at the Internet site below.

Address: Place Saint-Méen, 5660, Brûly-de-Pesche (Couvin)
Phone number: +32(0)60340140
Fax number: +32(0)60340143
E-mail: ot.couvin@scarlet.be
Website: www.couvin.be

France

Unlike her near neighbour, France has not embraced the fact that Hitler established a series of *Führerhauptquartiere* on her territory. Part of the reason for this is that Wolfsschlucht II near Margival, the largest and best preserved example, was used by NATO after the war and later as a training site for French commandos with access restricted. Although now disused,

One of the doors leading into the *Führerbunker* at Brûly-de-Pesche. The door is built in stable-door fashion so that if the bottom was blocked egress could still be gained through the top. In the distance is one of the wooden chalets, which serves today as a museum. (Author)

The original train station at Margival. Although Wolfsschlucht II is often quoted as being at Margival the actual *Führerbunker* is some 2km further up the track near the rail tunnel. Today the stop is still used, but not the station building. (Author)

the site is still fenced off and impromptu visits are actively discouraged. However, the site is opened to the public at certain times of the year. Further details can be found via the web site: http://w2margival.ifrance.com/

Moreover, around the headquarters there are many other bunkers and flak positions that can be visited. The site is also near Paris and some of the battlefields of World War I (the battle of the Aisne was fought along the Chemins des Dames), so it is eminently feasible to combine a trip to these places.

Germany
Understandably perhaps, little remains of the various *Führerhauptquartiere* in Germany. The bunkers of FHQ Adlerhorst were demolished after the war and the area redeveloped with the concrete bunkers sometimes used as the foundation for new buildings. Schloß Ziegenberg remains, and,

A roof section of one of the bunkers at Felsennest. It is possible to see the reinforcing rods used to strengthen the concrete and, at the bottom, the I-beams on which the roof sat. (Author)

although badly damaged in the war, it has been restored.

Führerhauptquartier Felsennest was also demolished and the area around it has seen significant changes, but, despite the fact that it is not advertised, the determined historian can still find vestiges of the bunkers outside the village of Rodert. Slightly farther south it is also possible to find remains of the bunkers at FHQ Tannenberg.

Sadly, despite the fact that it was witness to one of the most momentous events of the 20th century, the Führerbunker in Berlin was demolished and the remains buried, and today nothing is left to visit except a map of the bunkers.

In 1988 Hitler's bunker in Berlin was demolished to allow for the future development of the site that had sat unused since the end of the war. A number of historians were given permission to study the structures before they were buried for ever. (W. Fleischer)

Poland

The trauma suffered by Poland in the last century has had one positive result for the historian of fortifications; the country is home to a veritable cornucopia of treasures including Polish inter-war defences, Soviet bunkers of the Molotov Line and of course, arguably the pièce de résistance, three of Hitler's wartime *Führerhauptquartiere*. The most famous of these, FHQ Wolfsschanze, is located in the north of the country near Ketrzyn and is a popular tourist attraction. The facility was completely destroyed by the retreating Germans in January 1945, but the remains can still be visited. Some of the original buildings have been restored and are now used as a hotel and restaurant for visitors to the site. Nearby, the remains of the OKH headquarters 'Mauerwald' are much better preserved and are well worth a visit.

Farther to the south, near Lodz, is Anlage Mitte, (Tomaszów Mazowiecki) where an artificial tunnel was constructed for the Führer's train. It was never used by Hitler, but is still intact and can be viewed by the public. A similar facility was built at Stepina and is where Hitler met Mussolini in August 1941. Today the tunnel is used as a museum with a collection of Soviet and German militaria on show. Further details can be found at the Internet site (in Polish) below.

Address:	38-125, Stepina
Phone number:	602 76 06 76
E-mail:	militbogo@wp.pl
Website:	www.frysztak.pl/index.php?mgid=31

The disused rail tunnel at Strzyzów, which was adapted for Hitler's use, is also open to the public.

Führerhauptquartier Riese is in south-west Poland and is a massive complex. Parts of it are open to the public like the Osówka Complex, near Głuszyca, but many of the tunnels are dangerous and should not be visited without specialist equipment and local guides.

The entrance to Anlage Süd at Strzyzów. This is markedly different to the facility at Stepina. Rather than a man-made concrete shelter this was a tunnel bored into the hillside. Today it is sealed up but is open to the public at certain times. (Author)

Ukraine

Führerhauptquartier Wehrwolf, near Vinnitsa in Ukraine was destroyed before it was captured by the advancing Red Army. Today only the swimming pool and debris remain. Nevertheless, it was used extensively by Hitler in 1942–43 and for that reason alone it is of interest.

BIBLIOGRAPHY

WO219/819 – Location of Hitler's and Himmler's HQs (National Archives)

Baur, H., *Hitler At My Side* (Eichler Publishing Corporation: Texas, 1986)

Beevor, A., *Berlin: the Downfall, 1945* (Viking, 2002)

Below, N. von, *At Hitler's Side – The Memoirs of Hitler's Luftwaffe Adjutant 1937–45* (Greenhill Books: London, 2004)

Fest, J., *Inside Hitler's Bunker – The Last Days of the Third Reich* (Pan Books: London, 2005)

Focken, C., *Führerhauptquartier – Riese (Schlesien)* (Helios Verlag: Aachen, 2008)

——, *Führerhauptquartier – Wolfsschanze (Ostpreussen)* (Helios Verlag: Aachen, 2008)

Frenz, Walter, *Führerhauptquartier Wolfsschanze 1940–1945* (Arndt Verlag: Kiel, 2001)

Gross, M., *Bunkerstellungen der Luftverteidigungszone West im Rheinland und Hitlers Hauptquartier in Bad Münstereifel-Rodert* (Verlag W. Sünkel: Leinburg, 2001)

Hansen, Hans-Josef, *Felsennest – Das vergessene Führerhauptquartier in der Eifel* (Helios Verlag: Aachen, 2006)

Hoffmann, P., *Hitler's Personal Security – Protecting the Führer, 1921–1945* (Da Capo Press: USA, 2000)

Irving, D., *Hitler's War and The War Path* (Focal Point Publications: London, 2002)

Johnson, A. L., *Hitler's Military Headquarters – Organization, Structures, Security and Personnel* (R. James Bender Publishing: San Jose, California, 1999)

Junge, T., *Until the Final Hour – Hitler's Last Secretary* (Phoenix: London, 2004)

Lehmann, A. D., *In Hitler's Bunker – A Boy Soldier's Eyewitness Account of the Führer's Last Days* (Mainstream Publishing: Edinburgh, 2004)

Lehrer, S., *The Reich Chancellery and Führerbunker Complex* (McFarland & Company, Inc: Jefferson, North Carolina, 2006)

Loringhoven, B. F. von, *In the Bunker with Hitler – The Last Witness Speaks* (Weidenfeld & Nicolson: London, 2006)

Neumarker, U., Conrad, R. and Woywodt, C., *Wolfsschanze – Hitler's Machtzentrale im Zweiten Weltkrieg* (Ch Links Verlag: Berlin, 2007)

O'Donnell, J. P., *The Bunker* (Da Capo Press, 2001)

Rhode, P. and Sünkel, W., *Wolfsschlucht 2 – Autopsie eines Führerhauptquartiers* (Verlag W. Sünkel: Leinburg, 1995)

Schroeder, C., *He Was My Chief – The Memoirs of Adolf Hitler's Secretary* (Frontline Books: London, 2009)

Seidler, F. W. and Zeigert, D., *Hitler's Secret Headquarters* (Greenhill Books: London, 2004)

Speer, A., *Inside the Third Reich* (Weidenfeld and Nicolson: London, 1970)

Sünkel, W., Rack, R. and Rhode, P., *Adlerhorst – Autopsie eines Führerhauptquartiers* (Verlag W. Sünkel: Offenhausen, 2002)

Taylor, B., *Hitler's Headquarters – From Beer Hall to Bunker, 1920–1945* (Potomac Books, Inc.: Washington, DC, 2007)

Trevor-Roper, H., *The Last Days of Hitler* (Pan Books: London, 2002)

Warlimont, W., *Inside Hitler's Headquarters 1939–45* (Presidio Press: Novato, California, 1997)

Articles

Kühn, Dr. H. J., 'Die Vergessenen Führerhauptquartiere – Unvollendete Befehlszentren in Schlesien und Thüringen' in *IBA Informationen*, No. 22 (1993), pp. 34–47

Mollo, A., 'The Berlin Führerbunker: The Thirteenth Hole' in *After the Battle*, No. 61

Raiber, M. D., 'The Führerhauptquartiere' in *After the Battle*, No. 19

GLOSSARY

Dienststelle	Bureau
Doppelgruppenunterstand	Double Group Bunker
Flanders hedge	An obstruction constructed from stakes and barbed wire
Führer Begleit Bataillon	Führer Escort Battalion
Führersonderzug	Führer Special Train
Luftverteidigungszone West (LVZ West)	Air Defence Zone West
Nachrichtenbunker	Communication centre
Oberkommando des Heeres (OKH)	Army High Command
Oberkommando der Wehrmacht (OKW)	Armed Forces High Command
Reichsarbeitsdienst (RAD)	State Labour Service
Reichssicherheitsdienst (RSD)	Reich Security Service
Reichsaussenminister (RAM)	Reich Foreign Minister
Sperrkreis	Security Zone
SS Begleit Kommando	SS Escort Detachment
Wehrmachtführungsamt (WFA)	Precursor to WFSt
Wehrmachtführungsstab (WFSt)	Wehrmacht leadership staff

INDEX